The Caine Mutiny Court-Martial

The CAINE MUTINY COURT-MARTIAL

A DRAMA IN TWO ACTS

by Herman Wouk

based on his novel, "THE CAINE MUTINY"

NELSON DOUBLEDAY, INC.   GARDEN CITY, NEW YORK

This play is dedicated to
Charles Laughton
in admiration and gratitude.

NOTE

The Caine Mutiny Court-Martial is purely imaginary. No ship named U.S.S. *Caine* ever existed. The records show no instance of a U.S. Navy captain relieved at sea under Articles 184-186. The fictitious figure of the deposed captain was derived from a study of psychoneurotic case histories, and is not a portrait of a real military person or a type; this statement is made because of the existing tendency to seek lampoons of living people in imaginary stories. The author served under two captains of the regular Navy aboard destroyer-minesweepers, both of whom were decorated for valor. One technical note: court-martial regulations have been extensively revised since the Second World War. This trial takes place according to instructions then in force. Certain minor omissions have been made for purposes of brevity; otherwise the play strictly follows procedures stipulated in *Naval Courts and Boards*.

From the *Navy Regulations:*
Article 184. Unusual circumstances.

It is conceivable that most unusual and extraordinary circumstances may arise in which the relief from duty of a commanding officer by a subordinate becomes necessary, either by placing him under arrest or on the sick list; but such action shall never be taken without the approval of the Navy Department or other appropriate higher authority, except when reference to such higher authority is undoubtedly impracticable because of the delay involved or for other clearly obvious reason. Such reference must set forth all facts in the case, and the reasons for the recommendation, with particular regard to the degree of urgency involved.

Article 185. Conditions to fulfill.

In order that a subordinate officer, acting upon his own initiative, may be vindicated for relieving a commanding officer from duty, the situation must be obvious and clear, and must admit of the single conclusion that the retention of command by such commanding officer will seriously and irretrievably prejudice the public interests. The subordinate officer so acting must be next in lawful succession to command; must be unable to refer the matter to a common superior for one of the reasons set down in Article 184; must be certain that the prejudicial actions of his commanding officer are not caused by secret instructions unknown to the subordinate; must have given the matter such careful consideration, and must have made such exhaustive investigation of all the circumstances, as may be practicable; and finally must be thoroughly convinced that the conclusion to relieve his commanding officer is one which a reasonable, prudent, and experienced officer would regard as a necessary consequence from the facts thus determined to exist.

Article 186. Responsibility.

Intelligently fearless initiative is an important trait of military character, and it is not the purpose to discourage its employment in cases of this nature. However, as the action of relieving a superior from command involves most serious possibilities, a decision so to do or so to recommend should be based upon facts established by substantial evidence, and upon the official views of others in a position to form valuable opinions, particularly of a technical character. An officer relieving his commanding officer or recommending such action together with all others who so counsel, must bear the legitimate responsibility for, and must be prepared to justify, such action.

The Caine Mutiny Court-Martial had its first performance in the Granada Theatre, Santa Barbara, California, on October 12, 1953. After a tour across the United States it opened in New York at the Plymouth Theatre on January 20, 1954, with the same cast, as follows:

(In order of appearance.)

LT. STEPHEN MARYK	*John Hodiak*
LT. BARNEY GREENWALD	*Henry Fonda*
LT. COM. JOHN CHALLEE	*Ainslie Pryor*
CAPTAIN BLAKELY	*Russell Hicks*
LT. COM. PHILIP FRANCIS QUEEG	*Lloyd Nolan*
LT. THOMAS KEEFER	*Robert Gist*
SIGNALMAN THIRD CLASS JUNIUS URBAN	*Eddie Firestone*
LT. (JR. GRADE) WILLIS SEWARD KEITH	*Charles Nolte*
CAPT. RANDOLPH SOUTHARD	*Paul Birch*
DR. FORREST LUNDEEN	*Stephen Chase*
DR. BIRD	*Herbert Anderson*
STENOGRAPHER	*John Huffman*
ORDERLY	*Greg Roman*

SIX MEMBERS OF THE COURT: *Larry Barton, Jim Bumgarner, Stephen Scott, Richard Farmer, Richard Norris, Pat Waltz.*

ACT ONE: The Prosecution

ACT TWO: The Defense

The time of the play is February 1945. The scene is the General Court-Martial Room of the Twelfth Naval District, San Francisco. At the end of Act Two the scene shifts to a banquet room in the Hotel Fairmont, San Francisco.

Produced by Paul Gregory.

Directed by Charles Laughton.

DESCRIPTION OF CHARACTERS

GREENWALD: *A lanky lieutenant. His face is stern and abstracted.*

MARYK: *A big, powerfully built lieutenant, with close-cropped hair.*

CHALLEE: *A well set up lieutenant.*

BLAKELY: *A tall, white-haired captain.*

QUEEG: *Tanned, natty, erect; the picture of a correct naval officer. He is a short man in his thirties, with scanty hair.*

KEEFER: *A tall, clever-looking officer.*

URBAN: *A little sailor in blues.*

KEITH: *A handsome youngster with reddish-blond hair.*

SOUTHARD: *A dapper, lean officer. Close-cropped head; hard-bitten face.*

LUNDEEN: *Intelligent, plump man in his fifties; rimless glasses.*

BIRD: *A good-looking young lieutenant of the intellectual and ascetic type.*

COURT MEMBERS, STENOGRAPHER *and* ORDERLY *of varying types.*

All characters wear blues excepting GREENWALD, *who wears a green flier's uniform.*

The CAINE MUTINY COURT-MARTIAL

ACT ONE

The Prosecution

THE SCENE: *The Curtain is up when the audience enters the theater. Dimly visible is a gray-draped stage barren except for the chairs, tables, and witness box of a court-martial. The big raised curved judge's bench, Stage Right, is covered with green baize, and behind it on the draperies is a large American flag. Upstage Left is Lieutenant Commander Challee's desk. Next to his desk, placed out of the way, is Greenwald's desk, with two chairs placed on top. Behind, Upstage, is the witness stand: a chair on a raised round platform which rolls on casters. There is a chair for the Orderly, Stage Center, by the end of the judge's bench, and a chair and small desk for the Stenographer, Downstage Right, below Captain Blakely's place on the bench. The single entrance to the stage is through the curtains, deep Center Stage.*

The start of the play is marked by the dimming of the house LIGHTS and the brightening of the stage. The ORDERLY *and* STENOGRAPHER, *two sailors in dress blues, enter. They pick up* GREENWALD'S *desk and chairs, carry them Downstage Left, and put the chairs in place.* GREENWALD *enters, and as the* ORDERLY *and* STENOGRAPHER *roll the witness stand into place, Center Stage, he puts his briefcase down on his desk. Exit the two sailors.* GREENWALD, *a lanky lieu-*

tenant in a green flier's uniform with wings and campaign ribbons, strolls to the witness stand. His face is stern and abstracted. He stares at the stand for a few moments, then leans his elbows on the arms of the chair and puts his hand to his face. Enter MARYK, *a big, powerfully built lieutenant in blues, with close-cropped hair. He comes down to the other side of the witness stand and peers at* GREENWALD *for a moment.*

MARYK. What are they doing out there? This is a hell of a long recess— This is the longest recess yet.

GREENWALD. I've seen longer.

MARYK. I thought the trial would be over by now. All they do is swear in somebody, recess, look at a paper, recess, look at another paper, recess, mumble some legal words, recess some more—when does the court-martial start?

GREENWALD. Maryk, take it easy. It's going to be a long trial.

MARYK. But you won't tell me what you're doing, how you're going to conduct my case, what I'm supposed to say—nothing.

GREENWALD. It would only confuse you.

MARYK. I couldn't be more confused than I am.

GREENWALD. Well, you've got something there.

MARYK. I don't like the way you're handling me.

GREENWALD. Good. That makes us even.

MARYK. How's that?

GREENWALD. I don't like handling you.

MARYK. What? Well, then, maybe I'd better—

GREENWALD. (*Crossing to desk and taking papers from brief-case*) Maryk, I'd rather be prosecuting you than defending you. I told you that the first time we met. Nevertheless, I'm defending you. If it's humanly possible to win an acquittal in this case I'm going to win you an acquittal. If you want a prediction, I believe I'm going to get you off. But you can't help me, so just leave me be.

MARYK. You're a damn peculiar fish.

GREENWALD. My mother thinks I'm beautiful.

MARYK. That's a hell of a thing to say, you know.

GREENWALD. What?

MARYK. You'd rather be prosecuting me than defending me. How d'you suppose that makes me feel?

GREENWALD. (*Looks at him, crosses to him.*) You're nervous.

MARYK. Sure I am.

GREENWALD. I am too, a bit. Sorry.

MARYK. (*Looks up at him.*) I can ask the court for a different counsel.

GREENWALD. Forget it. I don't take on a case to lose it.

MARYK. You do think I was right to relieve Captain Queeg?

GREENWALD. I can't say that.

MARYK. After everything I told you, you still don't think he was nuts?

GREENWALD. No, I don't.

MARYK. Then I get hung.

GREENWALD. Not necessarily.

MARYK. Maybe I should plead guilty. Eight legal officers advised me to plead guilty. The court would go easy on me.

GREENWALD. I don't care if every legal officer in the Navy says otherwise, I think I can get you off.

MARYK. I'll get all fouled up.

GREENWALD. You'll do nobly. You may come out of this a great naval hero.

MARYK. (*Stares at him.*) Greenwald, is there something eating you?

GREENWALD. I don't know. (*Goes back to witness chair.*) I'm a damn good lawyer, Maryk, and I'm a pretty poor flyer. Took quite a shellacking at flight school from snotty ensign instructors four or five years younger than me. I didn't like it. Baby-faced kids couldn't do such things to Greenwald the hot shot lawyer. I used to daydream about a court-martial coming up on that base. And some poor Joe would need defending. And I'd step in, and take over, and twist the Navy's arm, and make it holler Uncle. Now—here's my dream come true. You know something? I don't look forward to twisting the Navy's arm. Not one bit.

MARYK. Scared of the brass, eh?

GREENWALD. Worse.

MARYK. What?

GREENWALD. Respectful.

MARYK. Listen, I put in for transfer to the regulars. I respect the Navy too.

GREENWALD. Maryk, they took us in naked. Just a lot of pink forked animals with belly buttons. And they worked us over, and kicked us around, and put us through a bunch of silly rituals, and stuffed us full of the dullest bloody books in the world, and slapped funny uniforms on us. And there we were all of a sudden with big flaming machines in our hands, sinking U-boats and shooting down Zeros. A lot of guys take it in stride. Me, it's sort of turned all my old ideas wrong side out. And this is a war that sure needs winning, for my dough.

MARYK. Well, I don't go along with you all the way.

GREENWALD. You don't.

MARYK. There's still a big pile of foolishness connected with the Navy. In fact—I sometimes think the Navy is a master plan designed by geniuses for execution by idiots.

GREENWALD. (*Startled.*) You think what?

MARYK. (*Self-conscious.*) The Navy is a master plan designed by geniuses for execution by idiots.

GREENWALD. Where'd you hear that?

MARYK. (*Injured.*) Couldn't I just have made it up?

GREENWALD. You could just have made up the Gettysburg Address, too. Where'd you hear it?

MARYK. (*Grins reluctantly.*) Well, matter of fact, it's one of Tom Keefer's favorite cracks.

GREENWALD. (*Nods.*) Ah yes. You echo your novelist friend quite a bit, don't you? (*Sits at desk.*)

MARYK. (*To desk*) Tom's got the keenest mind on the ship. About the keenest I've ever run into.

GREENWALD. He's keen, all right.

MARYK. I'm sure glad Tom is going to testify.

GREENWALD. You are?

MARYK. Hell! He knows everything Captain Queeg did. He knows psychiatry. I'm a stoop about those things. I'll foul myself up. Tom Keefer can tell the thing straight.

GREENWALD. If I had my way, Lieutenant Thomas Keefer would never appear in this court.

MARYK. What?

GREENWALD. He's not going to do you any good on the witness stand, Maryk, you mark my words. One man I'd really enjoy prosecuting is Mr. Thomas Keefer, the eminent novelist.

MARYK. (*Sits at desk.*) Greenwald, you're not to go pinning anything on Tom Keefer— It was my responsibility.

GREENWALD. That's right. You did what you did.
(*Enter the six* COURT MEMBERS, ORDERLY *and* STENOGRAPHER, *who take their places.*)
Well, here we go— It's better you did it out of your own noble judgment than that you took the advice of a sensitive novelist.

(CHALLEE *enters upstage, crosses to his desk, upstage Left. Puts his briefcase down, looks upstage to the entrance.*)

CHALLEE. Attention!

(ALL *stand to attention as* BLAKELY *enters and goes to his place in silence.*)

BLAKELY. We're spending excessive time in all these recesses. (*Rings bell.*)
(ALL *sit.*)
I appreciate the judge advocate's desire to have the record letter perfect. But let's get on with the case and hereafter keep technicalities to a minimum.

CHALLEE. Aye aye, sir.

BLAKELY. (*Holds out paper to* CHALLEE.) Court finds the charge and specification in due form and technically correct. Is the accused ready for trial?

(GREENWALD *motions to* MARYK *to rise.* MARYK *rises.* GREENWALD *sits.*)

MARYK. Yes, sir.

(BLAKELY *nods to* CHALLEE, *who reads from the paper.*)

CHALLEE. "Charge. Conduct to the prejudice of good order and discipline. Specification. In that Lieutenant Stephen

Maryk, U.S.N.R., did, on or about 18 December, 1944, aboard the U.S.S. *Caine*, willfully, without proper authority, and without justifiable cause, did relieve from his duty as commanding officer Lieutenant Commander Philip Francis Queeg, U.S.N., the duly assigned commanding officer of said ship, who was then and there in lawful exercise of his command, the United States then being in a state of war."—Stephen Maryk, lieutenant, United States Naval Reserve, you have heard the charge and specification preferred against you; how say you, guilty or not guilty?

MARYK. Not guilty.

GREENWALD. (*Rises.*) Accused admits he is Lieutenant Stephen Maryk, U.S.N.R., and that he was the executive officer of the U.S.S. *Caine* on December 18, 1944. (*Sits.*)

MARYK. (*Haltingly*) The admission is made with my authority.

BLAKELY. Judge advocate, present your case.

CHALLEE. (*To* ORDERLY.) Call Lieutenant Commander Queeg.

(*Exit* ORDERLY. *He returns in a moment with* QUEEG, *who is tanned, natty, erect, the picture of a correct naval officer.* CHALLEE *holds a Bible for him. He places left hand on it and raises right hand.*)

BLAKELY. (*Stands, raises his right hand.*) You do solemnly swear that the evidence you shall give in this court shall be the truth, the whole truth, and nothing but the truth, so help you God.

QUEEG. I do. (*Takes witness stand.*)

CHALLEE. State your name, rank, and present position.

QUEEG. Philip Francis Queeg, Lieutenant Commander, United States Navy, temporarily assigned to Commandant, Twelfth Naval District, awaiting reassignment by BuPers.

CHALLEE. If you recognize the accused, state as whom.

QUEEG. (*Glancing briefly at* MARYK) Lieutenant Stephen Maryk, U.S.N.R.

CHALLEE. Commander Queeg, on December 18, 1944, were you in command of the U.S.S. *Caine?*

QUEEG. I was.

CHALLEE. What type of vessel is the *Caine?*

QUEEG. Her official designation is high-speed minesweeper. What she is, is a four-piper, one of those flush deck twelve hundred ton destroyers from World War One, fixed up with minesweeping gear.

CHALLEE. An old ship, then?

QUEEG. I guess about the oldest type still doing combat duty.

CHALLEE. What is her primary mission?

QUEEG. (*Smiling*) That's a hard one. These old buckets are regarded as pretty expendable. By and large we were doing the usual destroyer duty—anti-submarine screening —also ran the mail, transported marines—carried aviation gas and torpedoes, gave fire support in minor landings, or what have you? Also swept mines now and then.

CHALLEE. Commander, on December 18, 1944, were you relieved of command of the *Caine?*

QUEEG. (*Slight pause.*) Yes.

CHALLEE. By whom?

QUEEG. By the accused.

CHALLEE. Was this a regular relief?

QUEEG. It was totally irregular, sir.

CHALLEE. How would you describe it?

QUEEG. Well, the most charitable description would be that it was an incident, a regrettable incident of temporary and total collapse of military discipline.

CHALLEE. Commander, please relate all the facts that bear on this unauthorized relief.

QUEEG. Kay, I'll try to do this consecutively, here. The *Caine* sortied from Ulithi Atoll on the sixteenth of December, I believe, the fifteenth or the sixteenth. We were a screening vessel with a group of fleet oilers. Our mission was to rendezvous with and refuel Admiral Halsey's fast carrier force in the Philippine Sea. Kay. Well, we made the rendezvous. And then this typhoon came along. The fueling was broken off and the fleet began to maneuver to evade the storm. Now, the storm was travelling due west— (*Gestures with hands.*) —so Admiral Halsey set fleet course due south and we began to make a run for the safe semicircle.

CHALLEE. What was the date and time of that course change?

QUEEG. That would be early morning of the eighteenth, sir. Well, as I say, the storm was pretty bad at this point. Visibility was almost zero. Couldn't see the guide or even the next ship in the screen, we were just steaming blindly through rain and spray. And of course with the wind and sea and all, we had to maneuver pretty smartly with engines and rudder to hold fleet course and speed. But we were doing fine. My executive officer, however, pretty early in the game began to show unusual symptoms of nervousness. And I had to—

CHALLEE. What were these symptoms of nervousness?

QUEEG. Well, for instance, he began talking very early—oh, it couldn't have been half an hour after the fleet started to run south—that we should operate independently and come around north.

CHALLEE. Why did he want to do that?

QUEEG. (*With illustrative gestures*) Well, to give you the picture on that—you see the typhoon was coming at us from the east. We were on the western edge of it. Now as you know these blows spin counter-clockwise above the equator. That means where we were the wind was from due north. Admiral Halsey, of course, was running south with the wind to get out of the storm's path. Now that's in accordance with all existing storm doctrine from Bowditch on up. But my exec insisted that the ship was on the verge of foundering, and we'd better come around and head into the wind—that is, north—if we were to survive. Of course we weren't in any such bad shape at all. And that's what I mean by nervousness.

CHALLEE. What was your objection to coming north, as the executive officer suggested?

QUEEG. Why, everything was wrong with that idea that could be wrong with it, sir. In the first place my orders were to proceed south. My mission was screening. My ship was in no danger and was functioning normally. Why, to drop out of station and act independently under those conditions was unthinkable. Coming around to north would have headed the ship directly into the heart of the typhoon. It was not only a senseless suggestion in the circumstances, it was almost suicidal. I might add that I've since checked my decisions of December eighteenth with the finest ship-handlers I know up to the rank of rear admiral, and they've unanimously agreed that the only course in that situation was south.

(CHALLEE *glances at* GREENWALD. *He is doodling obliviously.* CHALLEE *hesitates.*)

CHALLEE. Commander, your last remark was hearsay evidence. That is not acceptable.

QUEEG. Oh I'm sorry, sir. I'm not up on these legal distinctions as much as I should be, I guess.

CHALLEE. Perfectly all right.

(CHALLEE *and* BLAKELY *stare at* GREENWALD.)

BLAKELY. Will defense counsel move to strike out the part of the testimony which was hearsay evidence?

GREENWALD. (*Half rises.*) All right, sir. I so move. (*Sits.*)

CHALLEE. No objection.

(BLAKELY, *with a disgusted look at* GREENWALD, *turns to* STENOGRAPHER.)

BLAKELY. Strike out the last sentence.

CHALLEE. A ship-handling expert will be called, Commander, to testify on that point.

QUEEG. I see. I'm very glad to know that, sir. Thank you.

CHALLEE. Proceed with your description of the relief.

QUEEG. Kay. Well, it was just that Maryk kept insisting on coming north, more and more stridently as the weather deteriorated. Finally I began to be a little concerned about him. Then suddenly he walked up to me out of a clear sky, and told me I was on the sick list and he was relieving me. To be honest, I couldn't believe my ears, and was a little slow in catching on. It was only when he started shouting orders at the officer of the deck and countermanding my instructions to the helm that I began to realize what was going on.

CHALLEE. Commander, can you recall anything in your own bearing or manner that could have provoked your executive officer's act?

QUEEG. Well—truthfully, sir, I cannot. Frankly, I don't think my bearing or manner had anything to do with it. It was a pretty scary situation at the wheelhouse. The wind was force ten to twelve, screeching and all that, the waves were mountainous. The barometer was about as low as it's ever been in the U.S. Navy history. We took one very bad roll—and I mean a bad one, and I've done a lot of North Atlantic rolling, too—and I think Maryk simply went into panic.

CHALLEE. Was the *Caine* in grave danger at that moment?

QUEEG. Oh no, I wouldn't say that—no sir. We righted very nicely from that bad roll. He repeatedly tried to order me off the bridge, but I stayed right where I was. I gave him orders only when it seemed necessary for the safety of the ship. In the situation I thought the chief hazard was any further acts of frenzy on his part. And to the extent that the *Caine* did come safely through the storm despite this unprecedented running amuck of my executive officer, I believe my handling of the emergency was the correct one.

CHALLEE. Did Maryk cite any authority at all when he relieved you?

QUEEG. He mumbled something about Article 184. I didn't even catch it at the time. Later he said his authority was Articles one eighty-four, one eighty-five, and one eighty-six of the Naval Regulations.

CHALLEE. Are you familiar with these articles?

QUEEG. Certainly.

CHALLEE. In substance, what do they provide?

QUEEG. Well, as I understand it, they make it possible for an executive officer to take over in an emergency, a highly unusual emergency where the captain is—well, frankly, where the captain's gone absolutely and hopelessly looney.

CHALLEE. Were those Articles properly invoked in your situation?

QUEEG. (*Smiling wryly*) Well, I'm sort of an interested party here. But you won't have to take my word for it. I was successfully conning my ship through a typhoon. Fortunately there are a hundred thirty witnesses to that fact, every man who was aboard that ship.

CHALLEE. (*Glancing toward* GREENWALD) There again, sir, you're testifying to the conclusions of others.

QUEEG. (*Smiling*) Sorry. I'm obviously no legal expert. I'll withdraw that last sentence. (*With a glance at* BLAKELY.)

(BLAKELY *glances, annoyed, at* GREENWALD, *who seems to be paying no attention, doodling on a scratch pad.*)

BLAKELY. (*To* STENOGRAPHER) Strike the last sentence of the answer from the record.

CHALLEE. Have you ever been mentally ill, sir?

QUEEG. No, sir.

CHALLEE. Were you ill in any way when Mister Maryk relieved you?

QUEEG. I was not.

CHALLEE. Did you warn your executive officer of the consequences of his act?

QUEEG. I told him he was performing a mutinous act.

CHALLEE. What was his reply?

QUEEG. That he expected to be court-martialled, but was going to retain command anyway.

CHALLEE. What was the attitude of Lieutenant Junior Grade Keith, the officer of the deck?

QUEEG. He was in a state of panic as bad as Maryk's.

CHALLEE. What was the attitude of the helmsman?

QUEEG. Stilwell was emotionally unbalanced, and for some reason was very devoted to Mister Keith. They both backed up Maryk.

CHALLEE. (*Glances at the* COURT.) Is there anything else, Commander Queeg, that you care to state in connection with the events of 18 December aboard the *Caine?*

QUEEG. Well, I have thought a lot about it all, of course. It's the gravest occurrence in my career, and the only questionable one that I'm aware of. It was an unfortunate freak accident. If the O.O.D. had been anyone but this immature Keith, and the helmsman anyone but Stilwell, I don't think it would have happened. A competent officer of the deck would have repudiated Maryk's orders and a normal sailor at the helm would have disregarded both officers and obeyed me. It was just bad luck that those three men—Maryk, Keith and Stilwell—were combined against me at a crucial time. Bad luck for me, and I'm afraid worse luck for them.

(MARYK *writes a note to* GREENWALD, *who glances at it negligently, shakes his head and tears it up.*)

BLAKELY. The court would like to question the witness. Commander Queeg, you have taken all the prescribed physical and mental examinations incident to entrance to the Academy, graduation, commissioning, promotion, and so forth?

QUEEG. Yes, sir, for fourteen years.

BLAKELY. Does your medical record contain any history of illness, mental or physical?

QUEEG. It does not, sir. My tonsils were removed in the fall of nineteen thirty-eight.

BLAKELY. Have you ever had an unsatisfactory fitness report, Commander Queeg?

QUEEG. Negative, sir. I have one letter of commendation in my jacket.

BLAKELY. Now, Commander, can you account for Lieutenant Maryk's opinion that you were mentally ill?

QUEEG. (*Smiling*) Well—that's rather a tough one, sir.

BLAKELY. Well, I appreciate that, but it might be helpful.

QUEEG. Well, sir, I'll have to say that I assumed command of an extremely disorganized and dirty ship. Now that's no reflection on the officer I relieved. The *Caine* had had a year and a half of the most arduous combat duty, and it was understandable. Still, the safety of that ship and its crew demanded its being brought up to snuff. I took many stern measures. Lieutenant Maryk, I may say, from the first, didn't see eye to eye with me at all on this idea of making the *Caine* a taut ship again. Maybe he thought I was crazy to keep trying. I guess that's the picture, sir.

CHALLEE. No more questions. (*Sits*)

GREENWALD. (*Rises and approaches* QUEEG.) Commander Queeg, I should like to ask you whether you have ever heard the expression, "Old Yellowstain."

QUEEG. (*Looking genuinely puzzled*) In what connection?

GREENWALD. In any connection.

QUEEG. "Old Yellowstone"?

GREENWALD. "Old Yellowstain," sir.

QUEEG. I have not.

GREENWALD. You aren't aware, then, that all the officers of the *Caine* habitually referred to you as "Old Yellowstain"?

CHALLEE. (*Jumping to his feet*) I object to the question! It is impertinent badgering of the witness.

BLAKELY (*Frostily*) How does defense counsel Greenwald justify this line of questioning?

GREENWALD. If the court please, the nickname, "Old Yellowstain," used by the officers of the *Caine,* will be relevant to the issue of mental competence.

BLAKELY. (*Staring very hard at* GREENWALD) Before ruling, the court wishes to caution defense counsel. This is a most unusual and delicate case. The honor and career of an officer with an unblemished military record of fourteen years' standing is involved. The defense counsel will have to bear full responsibility for the conduct of his case.
(*Pause.*)
Subject to the foregoing comment, the judge advocate's objection is overruled. Court stenographer will repeat the question.

STENOGRAPHER. (*Tonelessly*) "You aren't aware then that all the officers of the *Caine* habitually referred to you as Old Yellowstain?"

QUEEG. I am not aware of it.

GREENWALD. No further questions at this time.

BLAKELY. Is that the extent of your cross-examination, Lieutenant Greenwald?

GREENWALD. Commander Queeg will be called as a witness for the defense, sir.

BLAKELY. For the *defense?*

GREENWALD. Yes, sir.

(BLAKELY *stares, shrugs, turns to* CHALLEE, *who shakes his head.*)

BLAKELY. (*To* QUEEG) Commander, you'll refrain from conversing with any person whatsoever concerning the details of your testimony today.

QUEEG. Aye aye, sir.

BLAKELY. You're excused, and thank you.

QUEEG. Thank you, Captain.

(QUEEG *exits.* ORDERLY *stands to attention.* COURT MEMBERS *all write notes.*)

CHALLEE. Call Lieutenant Thomas Keefer.

(*Exit* ORDERLY. KEEFER *enters, crosses down to* CHALLEE. *Puts hand on Bible.*)

BLAKELY. You do solemnly swear that the evidence you shall give in this court shall be the truth, the whole truth, and nothing but the truth. So help you God.

KEEFER. I do so swear.

(KEEFER *takes witness stand.* ORDERLY *re-enters, sits in his chair upstage.*)

CHALLEE. State your name, rank, and present station.

KEEFER. Thomas Keefer, Lieutenant U.S.N.R., communication officer of the U.S.S. *Caine.*

CHALLEE. If you recognize the accused, state as whom.

KEEFER. Steve Maryk, Lieutenant Stephen Maryk, executive officer of the *Caine.*

CHALLEE. What is your occupation in civilian life?

KEEFER. I'm a writer.

(GREENWALD *turns, looks at* KEEFER.)

CHALLEE. And has your work been published?

KEEFER. A number of my short stories have been published, yes, sir. (*To the* COURT.) In national magazines.

CHALLEE. Have you done any writing in your spare time while in service?

KEEFER. Yes, I've completed half a war novel.

CHALLEE. What is the title?

KEEFER. *Multitudes, Multitudes.*

BLAKELY. What was that?

KEEFER. *Multitudes, Multitudes,* sir.

BLAKELY. Oh. Thank you. (*Makes a note.*)

CHALLEE. And has this novel, *Multitudes, Multitudes,* though incomplete, recently been accepted by a New York publisher?

KEEFER. (*A little puzzled.*) Yes.

CHALLEE. I'm asking these questions to establish your reliability as an observer of personalities.

KEEFER. I understand, sir.

CHALLEE. Now, Lieutenant Keefer, were you serving aboard the *Caine* in your present capacity on December 18, 1944?

KEEFER. Yes sir.

CHALLEE. Was Captain Queeg relieved of command on that date?

KEEFER. He was, sir.

CHALLEE. By whom?

KEEFER. The accused.

CHALLEE. Describe how you learned that the captain had been relieved.

KEEFER. Well, Mister Maryk passed the word over the loudspeakers for all officers to lay up to the wheelhouse. When we got there he told us that the captain was sick and he had assumed command.

CHALLEE. Did Captain Queeg show any external signs of being sick?

(KEEFER *shifts in his seat and encounters* MARYK's *painfully intense glance.* MARYK *looks away angrily.*)

KEEFER. Well, at the height of a typhoon nobody aboard a four-piper looks very well—

(MARYK *reacts.* GREENWALD *writes a note.*)

CHALLEE. Was he raving, or foaming?

KEEFER. No.

CHALLEE. Did he look any worse than, say, Lieutenant Keith?

KEEFER. No, sir.

CHALLEE. Or Maryk?

KEEFER. We were all tired, dripping, and knocked out.

(MARYK *starts to move*, GREENWALD *passes him a note.* MARYK *turns away from* KEEFER.)

CHALLEE. Mister Keefer, did you make any effort to persuade Maryk to restore Queeg to command?

KEEFER. I did not.

CHALLEE. Didn't you feel the seriousness of the situation?

KEEFER. I certainly did, sir.

CHALLEE. Why did you take no remedial action?

KEEFER. I wasn't present when the captain was relieved. Maryk was in full command. The entire ship was obeying his orders. I decided that for the safety of the ship my best course was to obey his orders. That was what I did.

CHALLEE. Mister Keefer, were you aboard the *Caine* throughout the period when Captain Queeg was in command?

KEEFER. Yes.

CHALLEE. Did you ever observe any evidence of insanity in him?

(KEEFER *hesitates.* GREENWALD *turns in chair, looks at* KEEFER. MARYK *stretches his arms out in tension.*)

KEEFER. I don't—I can't answer that question, not being a psychiatrist.

(GREENWALD *puts his hand on* MARYK's *arm.* MARYK *pulls away.*)

CHALLEE. Well, surely now, Mister Keefer, as a writer you're not wholly ignorant of such matters.

KEEFER. (*Leans back in witness chair.*) Well, I hope not wholly ignorant,—no sir.

CHALLEE. What, for instance, is the Rorschach Test?

KEEFER. I believe that's the inkblot test. The analyst detects psychopathic tendencies in a person by showing him inkblots and getting the person to say what the shapes resemble.

CHALLEE. (*Nods.*) And who is Alfred Adler?

KEEFER. These things are very elementary. Adler split off from Freud. Any college man knows that much—sir.

CHALLEE. A novelist, however, is apt to understand and appreciate these things more than the average man.

KEEFER. Well, our work is the narration of human conduct.

(GREENWALD *turns, looks at* KEEFER, *then turns away, disgusted.*)

CHALLEE. Naturally. Now then, Mister Keefer, with your grasp of such matters—if you saw a man rushing up and down passageways screaming that a tiger was after him when there was no tiger, would you venture to say that that man was temporarily deranged?

KEEFER. (*Smiling wryly*) I would, sir.

CHALLEE. Did Commander Queeg ever exhibit such behavior?

KEEFER. No. Nothing like that.

CHALLEE. Did you ever think he might be insane?

(MARYK *frantically scribbles a note.*)

GREENWALD. (*Rising*) Objection. Witness isn't an expert. Matters of opinion are not admissible evidence.

(MARYK *pulls at* GREENWALD'S *sleeve, hands him a note.* GREENWALD *sits, reads note, then tears it up.*)

CHALLEE. (*With a slight smile*) I withdraw the question. Mister Keefer, at any time prior to 18 December were you informed that Maryk suspected Queeg of being mentally ill?

KEEFER. Yes sir.

CHALLEE. Describe how you learned this fact.

KEEFER. Well—now let me see—two weeks before the typhoon, Maryk showed me a medical log he'd kept on Queeg's behavior. He asked me to come with him to the *New Jersey* to report the situation to Admiral Halsey.

CHALLEE. Did you consent to go with him?

KEEFER. Yes, I did.

CHALLEE. Why?

KEEFER. He was my superior officer and also my close friend.

(MARYK *turns away.*)

CHALLEE. Did you believe that the log justified the relief of Queeg?

KEEFER. No—no, when we arrived aboard the *New Jersey*, I told him as forcibly as I could that in my opinion the log would not justify the action.

CHALLEE. What was his response?

KEEFER. Well, after a lot of arguing, he followed my advice. We returned to the *Caine*.

CHALLEE. Were you surprised, two weeks later, when he relieved the captain?

KEEFER. I was flabbergasted.

CHALLEE. Were you pleased, Mister Keefer?

KEEFER. I was badly disturbed. I anticipated that at best he would be involved in grave difficulties. I thought it was a terrible situation.

(MARYK *turns, rests head on hand.*)

CHALLEE. No further questions. (*Nods at* GREENWALD.)

GREENWALD. (*Half rises and then sits.*) No questions.

BLAKELY. Does the defense intend to recall the witness at a later time?

GREENWALD. No, sir.

BLAKELY. No cross-examination of this highly material witness?

GREENWALD. No, sir.

BLAKELY. The court will question the witness. Mister Keefer, now as to this so-called medical log. The facts it contained, which convinced Lieutenant Maryk that he should report the captain to Admiral Halsey, didn't convince you. Is that right?

KEEFER. They did not, sir.

BLAKELY. Why not?

KEEFER. Sir, it's not something a layman can intelligently discuss.

BLAKELY. You've stated you're a close friend of Mr. Maryk.

KEEFER. Yes, sir.

BLAKELY. This court is trying to find out among other things any possible extenuating circumstances for his acts. Did this medical log merely indicate to you that Captain Queeg was a highly normal and competent officer?

KEEFER. Sir, speaking from ignorance it's always seemed to me that mental disability was a relative thing. Captain Queeg was a very strict disciplinarian and extremely meticulous in hunting down the smallest matters. He was not the easiest person in the world to reason with. There were several occasions when I thought he bore down too hard and spent excessive time on small matters. Those were the things that were recorded in the medical log. They were very unpleasant. But to jump from them to a conclusion that the captain was a maniac—no—I was compelled in all honesty to warn Maryk against doing that.

BLAKELY. No further questions. You will not discuss your testimony outside this courtroom. Witness excused.

(KEEFER *steps down, turns, and walks out rapidly.* MARYK *looks after him.*)

CHALEE. Call Signalman Third Class Urban.

MARYK. (*Pulls* GREENWALD'S *arm.*) Why didn't you cross-examine Tom Keefer? Why did you let him off like that?

GREENWALD. It was the only thing to do.

MARYK. Why?

GREENWALD. It would have made things worse for you. You'll get your chance on the stand.

MARYK. I'll never say a word about Tom Keefer. Not me. God damn it, he should have talked himself.

GREENWALD. Sure he should. You don't understand, do you?
    (*Enter* URBAN, *crosses down to* CHALLEE, *puts hand on Bible.*)
Not about Keefer. Not even about yourself.

BLAKELY. (*Rises, raises right hand.*) You do solemnly swear that the evidence you shall give in this court shall be the truth, the whole truth, and nothing but the truth. So help you God.

URBAN. Aye aye, sir. (*Sits in witness chair.*)

(ORDERLY *re-enters, sits in his chair.*)

CHALLEE. State your name, rating, and present station.

URBAN. Junius Hannaford Urban, Signalman Third Class U.S.N., of the U.S.S. *Caine,* sir.

CHALLEE. If you recognize the accused, state as whom.

URBAN. Sir?

CHALLEE. Do you recognize the accused?

URBAN. Sir?

CHALLEE. (*Pointing*) Do you recognize the officer at that table?

URBAN. Which one, sir? There are two.

CHALLEE. Name the one you recognize.

URBAN. That's the exec, sir.

CHALLEE. What's his name?

URBAN. He's Mister Maryk.

CHALLEE. What is he exec of?

URBAN. The ship.

CHALLEE. Name the ship.

URBAN. The *Caine.*

CHALLEE. Thank you.

URBAN. Sorry, sir.

CHALLEE. Urban, on December 18, 1944, were you serving aboard the *Caine* in your present capacity?

URBAN. Is that the day it happened?

CHALLEE. The day what happened?

URBAN. I don't know.

CHALLEE. That was the day of the typhoon.

URBAN. Sure, I was aboard.

CHALLEE. Were you in the pilot house when Mister Maryk relieved Captain Queeg?

URBAN. Yes, sir.

CHALLEE. Who else was in the wheelhouse at that time?

URBAN. Well, there was the captain and Mister Maryk.

CHALLEE. Yes.

URBAN. And the helmsman.

CHALLEE. His name?

URBAN. Stilwell.

CHALLEE. Who else?

URBAN. The O.O.D.

CHALLEE. His name.

URBAN. Mister Keith.

CHALLEE. What were you doing in the wheelhouse?

URBAN. I had the watch, sir.

CHALLEE. Urban, describe in your own words how Lieutenant Maryk relieved the captain.

URBAN. He said, "I relieve you, sir."

CHALLEE. What was happening at the time?

URBAN. Well— The ship was rolling very bad.

CHALLEE. Urban, describe everything that happened in the ten minutes before Captain Queeg was relieved.

URBAN. Well, like I say, the ship was rolling very bad.

(*A long silence.* CHALLEE *waits, with his eyes on* URBAN.)

CHALLEE. That's all? Did the exec say anything? Did the captain say anything? Did the O.O.D. say anything? Did the ship just roll in silence for ten minutes?

URBAN. Well, sir, it was a typhoon.

BLAKELY. Urban, you're under oath.

URBAN. Well, I think the captain wanted to come north and the exec wanted to come south, or the other way around, or something like that.

CHALLEE. Why did the captain want to come south?

URBAN. I don't know, sir.

CHALLEE. Why did the exec want to come north?

URBAN. Sir, I'm a signalman.

CHALLEE. Did the captain act crazy?

URBAN. No, sir.

CHALLEE. Did the exec seem scared?

URBAN. No, sir.

CHALLEE. Did the captain?

URBAN. No, sir.

CHALLEE. Did anyone?

URBAN. *I* was goddamn scared, sir. (*To* BLAKELY) I beg your pardon, sir.

CHALLEE. But the captain did not act queer or crazy in any way at any time that morning—correct?

URBAN. The captain was the same as always, sir.

CHALLEE. (*Out of patience*) Crazy, or sane, Urban?

URBAN. He was sane, sir, so far as I knew.

BLAKELY. Urban, how old are you?

URBAN. Twenty, sir.

BLAKELY. What schooling have you had?

URBAN. One year in high school.

BLAKELY. Have you been telling the whole truth here or haven't you?

URBAN. Sir, the signalman isn't supposed to listen to arguments between the captain and the exec.

BLAKELY. Did you like the captain?

URBAN. (*Miserably*) *Sure* I liked him, sir.

BLAKELY. (*To* CHALLEE) Continue your examination.

CHALLEE. No further questions.

(CHALLEE *crosses up to his desk, sits.* GREENWALD *approaches the witness platform, rolling the pencil against his palm.*)

GREENWALD. Urban, were you aboard when the *Caine* cut her own tow cable the time she was towing targets outside Pearl Harbor?

URBAN. Yes, sir.

GREENWALD. What were you doing at the time that it happened?

URBAN. I was— That is, the captain was eating my— (*Catches himself just short of an obscenity, glances in horror at* BLAKELY.) —bawling me out—on the bridge, sir.

GREENWALD. What for?

URBAN. My shirttail was out.

GREENWALD. Was the captain very strict on the subject of shirttails?

URBAN. Sir he was a nut on—yes, sir. He was very strict on shirttails, sir.

GREENWALD. And while the captain was discussing your shirttail the ship went right around in a circle and steamed over its own towline? Is that the way it hap—

CHALLEE. (*Jumps up.*) Object to this line of questioning. Counsel has tricked the witness with leading questions into asserting as a fact that the *Caine* cut a towline, a material point that was not touched upon in direct examination.

GREENWALD. Please the court, the witness stated he had never seen the captain do anything crazy. I am attempting to refute this.

BLAKELY. Defense counsel will have the opportunity to originate evidence later. Objection sustained. Cross-examination thus far will be stricken from the record.

GREENWALD. Urban, what is a paranoid personality?

URBAN. Huh?

GREENWALD. What is a paranoid personality?

URBAN. Sir?

GREENWALD. Could you recognize a psychotic person?

URBAN. Me?

GREENWALD. No further questions. (*Crosses to desk and sits.*)

BLAKELY. Urban.
    (URBAN *rises.*)
    You will not discuss your testimony in this courtroom with anybody, understand?

URBAN. Who, sir? Me, sir? No, sir.

BLAKELY. Excused.

URBAN. Thank you, sir. (*Exits.*)

CHALLEE. Call Chief Water Tender Budge.

(ORDERLY *starts out.*)

GREENWALD. (*Rises.*) One moment.
(ORDERLY *halts.*)
If it please the court. I understand that the judge advocate intends to call a dozen members of the crew of the *Caine.*

CHALLEE. That's correct.

GREENWALD. Is the purpose to confirm the testimony of Urban that the captain was never seen to do anything crazy?

CHALLEE. That is the purpose.

GREENWALD. The defense will concede that the testimony of all these witnesses will corroborate Urban's—if the judge advocate will concede that these twelve men don't know any more about a paranoid than Urban.

CHALLEE. (*To* BLAKELY.) I'll gladly accept that concession on those terms, sir.

BLAKELY. Lieutenant Greenwald, you're making a weighty concession.

GREENWALD. By your leave, sir, however, the defense makes that concession. (*Sits.*)

BLAKELY. (*To* STENOGRAPHER.) One moment. Don't record that— Mister Greenwald.

GREENWALD. (*Stands.*) Yes, sir?

BLAKELY. The court understands that you were appointed as defense counsel by the judge advocate.

GREENWALD. Yes, sir.

BLAKELY. When were you appointed?

GREENWALD. Four days ago, sir.

BLAKELY. Do you feel you've had enough time to prepare your case?

GREENWALD. Yes, sir.

BLAKELY. Did you undertake this assignment willingly?

(GREENWALD *hesitates*.)

CHALLEE. (*Rises*.) May it please the court. Lieutenant Greenwald accepted the assignment at my earnest request.

BLAKELY. I see by your uniform that you're a flying officer.

GREENWALD. Yes, sir.

BLAKELY. What do you fly?

GREENWALD. F6F, sir.

BLAKELY. What are you doing on the beach? Were you grounded?

GREENWALD. Hospitalized for third degree burns, sir.

BLAKELY. (*A little more sympathetically*) I see. How did you get burned?

GREENWALD. Crashed a barrier on the U.S.S. *Wasp*, sir.

BLAKELY. Did you have a chance to practice much law before the war came along?

GREENWALD. (*Hesitantly*) A little, sir.

BLAKELY. Court will speak to the accused off the record.

(GREENWALD *sits, motions to* MARYK *to rise. He does.*)

MARYK. Yes, sir?

BLAKELY. It seems the court's duty at this point to inquire whether your counsel's conduct of the defense meets with your approval.

(MARYK *hesitates, looks from* GREENWALD *to* BLAKELY.)

GREENWALD. (*Rises*.) May it please the court. If the accused answers that question now he must do so on blind faith. I beg the court for an opportunity to speak to my client first.

BLAKELY. We've had too many recesses here.

GREENWALD. Not a recess, sir—a brief delay—two minutes, sir—

BLAKELY. Court will remain in session. We'll have a two minute pause in the proceedings. (*Rings the bell.*)

GREENWALD. Well, do you want to get rid of me?

MARYK. I don't know.

GREENWALD. Take my word for it. Everything's all right up to now.

MARYK. I think I'm sunk at this point.

GREENWALD. You're not.

MARYK. Fifteen years in the brig—

GREENWALD. You won't go to the brig.

MARYK. Why didn't you cross-examine these twelve guys?

GREENWALD. Two minutes isn't much time to explain elementary trial tactics.

MARYK. Explain one thing and maybe I'll go along with you. Why didn't you cross-examine Tom Keefer?

GREENWALD. Maryk, there isn't time to tell—

MARYK. Tom Keefer knows everything that the captain did. Everything!

GREENWALD. Sure he does.

MARYK. If he wouldn't talk it was up to you to drag it out of him. Wasn't it?

GREENWALD. You don't begin to understand.

MARYK. I don't understand what you're doing, mister, that's for sure.

GREENWALD. I just happen to want to fight this case.

MARYK. Why? What does it mean to you? You're a total stranger.

GREENWALD. I want to win it.

MARYK. I want to believe you.

GREENWALD. It's God's truth.

MARYK. You said you'd rather be prosecuting me than defending me. Maybe this is your screwy way of prosecuting me.

GREENWALD. All right. (*A harried glance at the Court and at his wrist watch.*) Listen carefully. Implicating Keefer harms you.

MARYK. What?

GREENWALD. Two disgruntled bastards instead of one heroic exec.
   (MARYK *stares, uncomprehending.*)
I've got a chance with a lone heroic exec. Making that picture stick is my only chance to win for you. Please try to let that sink in, Maryk.

(MARYK *keeps looking at him. Understanding slowly dawns on him as* CHALLEE *and* BLAKELY *talk.*)

BLAKELY. (*Motions to* CHALLEE *to come closer.*) Challee. (*In a confidential undertone*) What's going on here, Jack? Where'd you get this bird?

CHALLEE. Sir, Barney Greenwald and I went to Georgetown Law together. Before the war he was one of the most successful young lawyers in Washington.

BLAKELY. (*Staring at* GREENWALD) He was? Don't you think he is putting up a damned queer show?

CHALLEE. Well, yes, sir— But he has a reputation for defending the underdog, sir. He used to handle Indian cases back in Washington—

(GREENWALD *rises and puts his hand on* MARYK's *shoulder.*)

—where Indians were getting pushed around by the officials—and didn't charge for it.

BLAKELY. Jewish fellow, isn't he?

CHALLEE. Yes, sir. Barney's Jewish.

BLAKELY. Well, maybe he's a hell of a lot smarter than he seems. (BLAKELY *rings bell.*)

(MARYK *rises.* GREENWALD *crosses back to his chair.*) The court again asks the accused—are you satisfied?

MARYK. (*After a long stare at* GREENWALD, *shakily*) I'm satisfied, sir.

BLAKELY. Court will not reopen this question.

MARYK. I understand, sir. I'm satisfied with Lieutenant Greenwald.

BLAKELY. (*Nods to* CHALLEE.) Proceed with your case, Commander Challee.

CHALLEE. Call Lieutenant Keith.

(ORDERLY *goes.* LT. (J.G.) WILLIS KEITH *enters.* CHALLEE *holds Bible for him.*)

BLAKELY. You do solemnly swear that the evidence you shall give in this court shall be the truth, the whole truth, and nothing but the truth. So help you God.

KEITH. I do.

(KEITH *takes the stand.* ORDERLY *re-enters, sits.*)

CHALLEE. State your name, rank, and present station.

KEITH. Willis Seward Keith, Lieutenant Junior Grade U.S.N.R., Assistant Communication Officer of the U.S.S. *Caine.*

CHALLEE. If you recognize the accused, state as whom.

KEITH. Steve Maryk, my executive officer on the *Caine*.

CHALLEE. Mister Keith, were you officer of the deck of the *Caine* during the forenoon watch on 18 December, 1944?

KEITH. I was.

CHALLEE. Was the captain relieved of his command during your watch?

KEITH. Yes.

CHALLEE. Do you know why the executive officer relieved the captain?

KEITH. Yes. Captain Queeg had lost control of himself and the ship was in grave danger of foundering.

CHALLEE. How many years have you served at sea, Lieutenant?

KEITH. One year and three months.

CHALLEE. Do you know how many years Commander Queeg has served at sea?

KEITH. I guess about ten years.

CHALLEE. Which of you is better qualified to judge whether a ship is foundering or not?

KEITH. Myself, sir, if I'm in possession of my faculties and Commander Queeg isn't.

CHALLEE. What makes you think he isn't in possession of his faculties?

KEITH. He wasn't on the morning of December eighteen.

CHALLEE. Have you studied medicine or psychiatry?

KEITH. No.

CHALLEE. Did the captain foam, or rave, or make insane gestures?

KEITH. No, but what he did do was just as bad.

CHALLEE. Clarify that a bit, if you will.

KEITH. His orders were vague and sluggish and—not appropriate. He insisted on going south, when we had a north wind of ninety miles an hour behind us. With a stern wind that strong the ship couldn't be controlled.

CHALLEE. In your expert opinion as a ship-handler, that is.

KEITH. Steve Maryk thought so, and he's an expert ship-handler.

CHALLEE. Were you wholeheartedly loyal to your captain or antagonistic to him, prior to 18 December?

KEITH. I was antagonistic to Captain Queeg at certain isolated times.

CHALLEE. At what isolated times were you antagonistic?

KEITH. When Captain Queeg maltreated the men, I opposed him.

CHALLEE. When did the captain ever maltreat the men?

KEITH. Well, for one thing he systematically persecuted Gunner's Mate Second Class Stilwell.

CHALLEE. In what way?

KEITH. First he restricted him to the ship for six months for reading on watch. He refused to grant him leave in the States when we were back here in December '43. The man was getting anonymous letters about his wife's infidelity. Maryk gave Stilwell a seventy-two-hour emergency leave and he returned a few hours over leave and—

CHALLEE. You say Maryk gave Stilwell a pass. Did Maryk know that the captain had denied leave to Stilwell?

KEITH. Yes sir.

CHALLEE. Did Maryk check with the captain before issuing this pass?

KEITH. No sir.

CHALLEE. Are you testifying, Mister Keith, that Maryk deliberately violated his captain's orders?

KEITH. (*Rattled.*) Well, I mean it was my fault, actually. I begged him to. I was morale officer, and I thought the man's morale—I mean—

CHALLEE. Mister Keith, we now have your testimony, that you and Maryk and Stilwell connived to circumvent an express order of your commanding officer, a whole year before the typhoon of 18 December— Now, please tell the court any other instances of maltreatment that occur to you.

KEITH. (*Pause.*) He cut off the movies for six months just because he wasn't invited to a showing by mistake—he cut off the water at the equator because he said the men were using too much and had to be taught a lesson—

CHALLEE. Mister Keith, did the captain ever issue rules or punishments not permitted by regulations?

KEITH. He never did anything not allowed by regulations.

CHALLEE. You didn't like the captain, did you, Lieutenant?

KEITH. I did at first, very much. But I gradually realized that he was a petty tyrant and utterly incompetent.

CHALLEE. Did you think he was insane, too?

KEITH. Not until the day of the typhoon.

CHALLEE. Very well, come to the day of the typhoon. Was your decision to obey Maryk based on your judgment that the captain had gone mad or was it based on your hatred of Captain Queeg?

KEITH. (*Miserably, after a betraying pause and glance at* MARYK) I just don't remember my state of mind that long ago.

CHALLEE. (*Contemptuously*) No further questions. (*Turns on his heel and sits down.*)

GREENWALD. (*Rises.*) Mister Keith, you have stated you disliked Captain Queeg.

KEITH. I did dislike him.

GREENWALD. Did you state under direct examination all your reasons for disliking him?

KEITH. Not at all.

GREENWALD. State the rest of your reasons now, please.

KEITH. Well, for one thing, he extorted a hundred dollars from me—

CHALLEE. (*Rises.*) Objection. The issue in this case is not whether Captain Queeg was a model officer, but whether he was insane on 18 December. Defense counsel hasn't even touched this issue.

GREENWALD. Please the court, this will bear directly on the mental fitness of Captain Queeg to command a naval vessel, and as evidence it is nothing but clarification of Keith's dislike of his commanding officer, a fact established by the judge advocate at great pains in direct examination.

BLAKELY. The objection is overruled.

(CHALLEE *sits.*)

GREENWALD. Describe this so-called extortion, Mister Keith.

KEITH. Well, this was back last December in San Francisco Bay. The captain had this big crate full of cheap tax free whiskey from Pearl Harbor that he wanted to sneak into Oakland. He appointed me boat officer, and a working party started to load the crate into the gig. It was terrifically heavy and Captain Queeg got excited and screeched a whole bunch of contradictory orders. The sailors got rattled and dropped the crate into the water. It sank like a stone. And I was out a hundred and ten dollars.

GREENWALD. You mean the captain was?

KEITH. No, sir, I was—the captain informed me that I was responsible because I was boat officer in charge of the loading and he asked me to think over what I ought to do about it. Well, I was supposed to go on leave the next day, my girl had flown out from New York to be with me, so I went to the captain and I apologized for my stupidity and said I'd like to pay for the lost crate. He took my money gladly and then he signed my leave papers.

GREENWALD. What further reason did you have for disliking Queeg?

KEITH. (*A pause to gather his nerve.*) My chief reason for disliking Captain Queeg was his cowardice in battle.

GREENWALD. What cowardice?

KEITH. He repeatedly ran from shore batteries—

CHALLEE. (*Rises. Infuriated.*) Objection! Counsel is originating evidence beyond the scope of direct examination. He is leading the witness into irresponsible libels of an officer of the Navy.

(BLAKELY *starts looking through Naval Regulations.*)

GREENWALD. Please the court, the witness's dislike of Queeg was not only in the scope of direct examination, it was the key fact brought out. The witness has confessed ignorance of psychiatry. Things Queeg did, which caused the witness in his ignorance to dislike him, may in fact have been the helpless acts of a sick man.

CHALLEE. I respectfully urge my objection, sir.

BLAKELY. One moment.
   (COURT MEMBERS *write ballots.*)
For the benefit of all parties, court will read from the Articles for the Government of the Navy on cowardice.

(*Reads.*) "The punishment of death, or such other punishment as a court martial may adjudge, may be inflicted on any person in the naval service, who in time of battle, displays cowardice, negligence, or disaffection, or withdraws or keeps out of danger to which he should expose himself—"

(COURT MEMBERS *pass ballots to* BLAKELY.)

The defense counsel and the witness are warned that they are on the most dangerous possible ground. In charging an officer of the United States Navy with an offense punishable by death and that the most odious offense in military life, they take on themselves the heaviest responsibility. The court now asks defense counsel in view of the foregoing whether he desires to withdraw his question.

GREENWALD. I do not so desire, sir.

BLAKELY. The court asks the witness to state whether he desires to withdraw his answers.

KEITH. I do not so desire, sir.

BLAKELY. (*With icy gravity*) Court finds that the question is within the scope of direct examination, and that the answer is material. The objection of the judge advocate is overruled. (*Tears ballots.*)

(CHALLEE *sits.*)

(*Nods to* GREENWALD.) Proceed.

GREENWALD. Where and when did Captain Queeg run from shore batteries?

KEITH. Practically every time we heard gunfire from the beach. I guess the worst time was at Kwajalein. That's where he got the nickname, "Old Yellowstain."

GREENWALD. What did this nickname "Old Yellowstain" imply?

KEITH. Well, cowardice, of course. It referred to a yellow dye marker he dropped over the side.

GREENWALD. Describe this Yellowstain incident.

KEITH. Well, I wasn't on the bridge, so I only heard about it afterwards. What happened was that Captain Queeg—

CHALLEE. (*Rises.*) Objection. Does defense counsel seriously expect to enter these hearsay libels on the record?

GREENWALD. I withdraw the question. Defense will introduce direct evidence on the Yellowstain incident.

(CHALLEE *sits.*)

BLAKELY. Strike the question and answer from the record.

GREENWALD. Can you describe incidents of cowardice to which you were an eye witness?

KEITH. Well, in any combat situation Captain Queeg was always found on the side of the bridge away from the firing. I saw that a dozen times when I was O.O.D.

GREENWALD. No further questions. (*Goes to his seat.*)

CHALLEE. (*Rises.*) Mister Keith, has Commander Queeg been court-martialled by higher authority for any of the alleged acts of cowardice you describe?

KEITH. No.

CHALLEE. Can you cite any official records that will substantiate any of these fantastic and libelous stories you have been telling under the guidance of defense counsel?

KEITH. Official records? No.

CHALLEE. Mister Keith, do you know for a fact that the crate that was lost contained smuggled liquor?

KEITH. It was common knowledge.

CHALLEE. Common knowledge. Did you see the liquor in the crate?

KEITH. No—

CHALLEE. Can you name one person who will testify that they saw liquor in the crate?

KEITH. Well, naturally, he was pretty careful about that.

CHALLEE. Not one person.

KEITH. I just don't know who would have actually seen it.

CHALLEE. Mister Keith, you've testified that you hate Captain Queeg. You're reporting as fact every evil rumor about him and you're making wild irresponsible charges under oath. Isn't that the plain truth about your testimony, Mister Keith?

KEITH. I haven't lied once.

CHALLEE. Mister Keith, on the morning when the Captain was relieved, did you really think he had gone crazy?

KEITH. I said before I can't say for sure what my state of mind was.

CHALLEE. No more questions.

(BLAKELY *looks at* GREENWALD, *who shakes his head.*)

BLAKELY. (*To* KEITH.) You'll not discuss any details of your testimony outside this courtroom, Lieutenant.

KEITH. Aye aye, sir.

BLAKELY. You're excused.

(*Exit* KEITH, *with a glance at* MARYK *and a slight despairing shrug.*)

CHALLEE. Call Captain Southard.

(*Exit* ORDERLY, *returning with a dapper, lean officer. Close-cropped head, hard-bitten face, three rows of ribbons and stars. Business with Bible.*)

BLAKELY. You do solemnly swear that the evidence you shall give in this court shall be the truth, the whole truth and nothing but the truth. So help you God.

SOUTHARD. I do. (*Takes the witness chair.*)

CHALLEE. State your name, rank, and present station.

SOUTHARD. Randolph Patterson Southard, Captain U.S. Navy, Commander, Destroyer Squadron Eight.

CHALLEE. You understand that you've been called as an expert witness on destroyer ship-handling?

SOUTHARD. I do.

CHALLEE. State your qualifications.

SOUTHARD. Some twenty years in destroyers. Ten years of commanding all types, from the World War One four-piper on up to the newest twenty-two-hundred tonner.

CHALLEE. Now, sir, I'm going to describe a hypothetical ship-handling problem for your expert opinion.

SOUTHARD. Very well.

CHALLEE. You're in command of a destroyer in the Philippine Sea. A typhoon blows up without warning, travelling west. You're directly in the path of it. The wind keeps increasing, its direction holding steady from the north. Soon your wind is force ten to twelve and your seas are mountainous. Under the circumstances, what would you do?

SOUTHARD. I believe I'd execute the classic Navy maneuver known as getting the hell out of there.

CHALLEE. How would you go about that, Captain?

SOUTHARD. Well, it's almost rule of thumb. You say the wind's from the north at ninety knots, the center of the typhoon coming at you from the west. Best course is south. You might have to head a couple of points one way or the other, depending on your seas, but there's only one way out of that mess—south.

CHALLEE. But then you have a terribly strong stern wind, don't you?

SOUTHARD. What about it?

CHALLEE. Can a destroyer ride safely going downwind in such conditions?

SOUTHARD. She'll ride just as well going downwind as upwind. In fact, with your high freeboard forward, a destroyer tends to back into the wind. Other things being equal, she'll do slightly better going downwind.

CHALLEE. How about turning north in those circumstances and heading into the wind?

SOUTHARD. That would be dubious and dangerous, not to say idiotic.

CHALLEE. Why, Captain?

SOUTHARD. You're heading yourself right back into the path of the typhoon. Unless you're interested in sinking, that's not smart.

CHALLEE. That's all, sir. (*Crosses to his desk and sits.*)

GREENWALD. (*Rises.*) Captain, have you ever conned a ship through the center of a typhoon?

SOUTHARD. Negative. Been on the fringes often but always managed to avoid the center.

GREENWALD. Have you ever commanded a destroyer-minesweeper, sir?

SOUTHARD. Negative.

GREENWALD. This case, sir, concerns a destroyer-minesweeper at the center of a typhoon—

SOUTHARD. (*Frostily*) I'm aware of that. I've had DMS's under my command in screens, and I've read the book on 'em. They don't differ from destroyers except in details of topside weight characteristics.

GREENWALD. I ask these questions, Captain, because you are the only expert witness on ship-handling, and the extent of your expert knowledge should be clear to the court.

SOUTHARD. That's all right. I've handled destroyer types in almost every conceivable situation for ten years. Haven't handled a DMS at the center of a typhoon, no, but I don't know who the hell has besides the skipper of the *Caine*. It's a thousand-to-one shot.

GREENWALD. Will you state without reservation that the rules of destroyer handling would hold for a DMS in the center of a typhoon?

SOUTHARD. Well, at the center of a typhoon there are no hard-and-fast rules. That's one situation where it's all up to the commanding officer. Too many things happen too fast.

GREENWALD. Sir, you remember the hypothetical question of the judge advocate about the typhoon.

SOUTHARD. I do.

GREENWALD. Now in that situation, I ask you to assume that the winds and seas become worse than any you've ever experienced. Your ship is wallowing broadside. You actually believe your ship is foundering. You're in the last extremity. Would you bring your ship north, into the wind, or continue on south stern to wind?

SOUTHARD. You're getting mighty hypothetical.

GREENWALD. Yes, sir. You'd prefer not to answer that question, Captain?

SOUTHARD. I'll answer it. In the last extremity I'd come around to north and head into the wind, if I could, but *only* in the last extremity.

GREENWALD. Why, sir?

SOUTHARD. Why, because your engines and rudder have the best purchase that way, that's all. It's your last chance to keep control of your ship.

GREENWALD. But wouldn't coming north head you back into the path of the storm?

SOUTHARD. First things first. If you're on the verge of foundering you're as bad off as you can get. Mind you, you said the last extremity.

GREENWALD. Yes, sir, no further questions. (*Sits.*)

CHALLEE. (*Rises.*) Captain, who in your opinion is the best judge as to whether a ship is in its last extremity?

SOUTHARD. There's only one judge. The commanding officer.

CHALLEE. Why, sir?

SOUTHARD. The Navy's made him captain because his knowledge of the sea and of ships is better than anyone else's on the ship. It's very common for some subordinate officers to think the ship is sinking when all they're having is a little weather.

CHALLEE. Don't you think, sir, that when his subordinates all agree that the ship is going down the captain ought to listen to them?

SOUTHARD. Negative! Panic is a common hazard at sea. The highest function of command is to override it and to listen to nothing but the voice of his own professional judgment.

CHALLEE. Thank you Captain. (*Sits.*)

BLAKELY. (*With the smile of an old friend at* SOUTHARD) You will not discuss your testimony outside the courtroom, Captain.

SOUTHARD. Understood.

BLAKELY. You're excused, and thank you.

(*Exit* SOUTHARD.)

CHALLEE. Call Doctor Forrest Lundeen.

(*Exit* ORDERLY. *Returns with* LUNDEEN. *Bible business.*)

BLAKELY. You do solemnly swear that the evidence you shall give in this court shall be the truth, the whole truth and nothing but the truth. So help you God.

LUNDEEN. I do. (*Takes stand.*)

CHALLEE. State name, rank, and present station.

LUNDEEN. Forrest Lundeen, M.D., Captain U.S. Navy. Head of psychiatry, U.S. Naval Hospital, San Francisco.

CHALLEE. Were you the head of the medical board which examined Lieutenant Commander Queeg?

LUNDEEN. I was.

CHALLEE. How long did your examination last, Doctor?

LUNDEEN. We had the commander under constant observation and testing for three weeks.

CHALLEE. What was the finding of the board?

LUNDEEN. Commander Queeg was discharged with a clean bill of health.

CHALLEE. Doctor, is it possible that two months ago, on December 18, he was in such a state of psychotic collapse that relieving him from a naval command would be justified?

LUNDEEN. It's utterly impossible.

CHALLEE. Is it possible for a sane man to perform offensive, disagreeable, foolish acts?

LUNDEEN. It happens every day. We didn't find that the commander was a perfect officer.

CHALLEE. Yet you still say that to relieve him from naval command because of mental illness would be unjustified?

LUNDEEN. Completely unjustified.

CHALLEE. We will place your report in evidence and hear Doctor Bird. Thank you, Doctor.

(CHALLEE *glances directly into* GREENWALD's *eyes, with a thin cold grin.* GREENWALD *shuffles toward witness platform, rubbing his nose with the back of his hand, looking down at his feet, and presenting a general picture of flustered embarrassment.*)

GREENWALD. Doctor Lundeen, my background is legal, not medical. I hope you'll bear with me if I try to clarify technical terms.

LUNDEEN. Of course, of course.

GREENWALD. I'll probably ask some elementary questions.

LUNDEEN. Perfectly all right.

GREENWALD. Would you say that Commander Queeg is absolutely normal?

LUNDEEN. Well, normality, you know, is a fiction in psychiatry. No adult is without problems except a happy imbecile.

GREENWALD. Describe Commander Queeg's problems.

LUNDEEN. Well, you might say the over-all problem is one of inferiority feelings generated by an unfavorable childhood and aggravated by certain adult experiences.

GREENWALD. Unfavorable childhood in what way?

LUNDEEN. Disturbed background. Divorced parents, financial trouble, schooling problems.

GREENWALD. And the aggravating factors in adult life?

LUNDEEN. (*Hesitant.*) In general, the commander is rather troubled by his short stature, his low standing in his class and such factors. The commander is well adjusted to all these things.

GREENWALD. Can you describe the nature of the adjustment?

LUNDEEN. Yes, I can. His identity as a naval officer is the essential balancing factor. It's the key to his personal security. Therefore he has a fixed anxiety about protecting his standing. That would account for the harshness and ill-temper.

GREENWALD. Would he be disinclined to admit to mistakes?

LUNDEEN. Yes. Of course there's nothing unbalanced in that.

GREENWALD. Would he be a perfectionist?

LUNDEEN. Such a personality would be.

GREENWALD. Suspicious of his subordinates? Inclined to hound them about small details?

LUNDEEN. Any mistake of a subordinate is intolerable because it might endanger him.

GREENWALD. Yet he will not admit mistakes when he makes them himself.

LUNDEEN. You might say he revises reality in his own mind so that he comes out blameless.

GREENWALD. Doctor, isn't distorting reality a symptom of mental illness?

LUNDEEN. It's a question of degree. None of us wholly faces reality.

GREENWALD. But doesn't the commander distort reality more than, say, you do?

LUNDEEN. That's his weakness. Other people have other weaknesses. It's definitely not disabling.

GREENWALD. If criticized from above, would he be inclined to think he was being unjustly persecuted?

LUNDEEN. It's all one pattern, all stemming from one basic premise, that he must try to be perfect.

GREENWALD. Would he be inclined to stubbornness?

LUNDEEN. Well, you'll have a certain rigidity of personality in such an individual. The inner insecurity checks him from admitting that those who differ with him may be right.

GREENWALD. (*Suddenly switching from the fumbling manner to clicking preciseness.*) Doctor, you've testified that the following symptoms exist in the commander's behavior: rigidity of personality, feelings of persecution, unreasonable suspicion, withdrawal from reality, perfectionist anxiety, an unreal basic premise, and an obsessive sense of self-righteousness.

LUNDEEN. (*Looking startled, then amused.*) All mild, sir, all well compensated.

GREENWALD. Yes, Doctor. Is there an inclusive psychiatric term—one label—for this syndrome?

LUNDEEN. Syndrome? Who said anything about a syndrome? You're misusing a term. There's no syndrome, because there's no disease.

GREENWALD. Thank you for the correction, Doctor. I'll rephrase it. Do the symptoms fall into a single pattern of neurotic disturbance—a common psychiatric class?

LUNDEEN. I know what you're driving at of course. It's a paranoid personality, but that is not a disabling affliction.

GREENWALD. What kind of personality, Doctor?

LUNDEEN. Paranoid.

GREENWALD. Paranoid, Doctor?

LUNDEEN. Yes, paranoid.

(GREENWALD *glances at* CHALLEE, *then looks around slowly one by one at the faces of the* COURT MEMBERS. *He starts back to his desk.* CHALLEE *rises. A moment of silence.* GREENWALD *shuffles papers at his desk.* CHALLEE *sinks into his seat.*)

GREENWALD. Doctor, in a paranoid personality like Commander Queeg's—well, let me put this hypothetically. Could a man have a paranoid personality which would not disable him for any subordinate duties, but would disable him for command?

LUNDEEN. (*Rather irritated.*) It's conceivable.

GREENWALD. Is the disabling factor likely to show up in personal interviews?

LUNDEEN. With a skilled psychiatrist, yes.

GREENWALD. Why is a psychiatrist needed, Doctor? Can't an educated intelligent person, like myself, or the judge advocate, or the court, detect a paranoid?

LUNDEEN. (*Sarcastically*) You evidently are not too well acquainted with the pattern. The distinguishing mark of this neurosis is extreme plausibility and a most convincing normal manner on the surface. Particularly in self-justification.

GREENWALD. Thank you, Doctor. No more questions. (*Sits.*)

(*The* COURT MEMBERS *look tensely at* BLAKELY.)

BLAKELY. The court wishes to clear up one point. Doctor, is such a thing possible? (*Hesitates.*) Well, let me put it this way. Let's say a man with a mild condition is not disabled for all the usual stresses of command. Now let's say the stresses are multiplied manifold by an extreme emergency. Would there be a tendency to make erroneous judgments?

LUNDEEN. Well, there might be. Extreme stress does that to almost anybody, sir.

BLAKELY. (*Sternly*) It's not supposed to do it to commanding officers.

LUNDEEN. No, but practically speaking sir, they're human, too.

BLAKELY. You are not to discuss your testimony outside the courtroom. You're excused.

LUNDEEN. Yes, sir.

BLAKELY. Thank you, Doctor.

(*Exit* LUNDEEN.)

CHALLEE. Doctor Bird will be my last witness, sir.

(CHALLEE *nods to* ORDERLY. *Exit* ORDERLY, *returning with* BIRD. *Bible business.*)

BLAKELY. You do solemnly swear that the evidence you shall give in this court shall be the truth, the whole truth, and nothing but the truth. So help you God.

BIRD. I do. (*Takes the stand.*)

CHALLEE. State your name, rank, and present station.

BIRD. Allen Winston Bird, M.D., Lieutenant U.S.N.R. On the psychiatric staff of U.S. Naval Hospital, San Francisco.

CHALLEE. Were you a member of the board headed by Doctor Lundeen which recently inquired into the mental health of Lieutenant Commander Queeg?

BIRD. Yes, sir.

CHALLEE. What was the finding of the board?

BIRD. We found that the commander is mentally fit for command now and has never been unfit.

CHALLEE. (*After a pause.*) Did you find any indication that Commander Queeg had what is known as a paranoid personality?

BIRD. Well, I prefer to call it obsessive personality with paranoid features.

CHALLEE. But this did not indicate mental unfitness however?

BIRD. Oh, no.

CHALLEE. You unanimously agreed, then, Doctor, that Commander Queeg is mentally fit now and must have been mentally fit on 18 December, when he was relieved on the grounds of mental illness?

BIRD. That was our unanimous conclusion.

CHALLEE. Thank you, Doctor. No further questions.

GREENWALD. (*Appraises* BIRD *with a cold eye, slowly gets out of his chair, and approaches him.*) Doctor, you have special training in Freudian technique?

BIRD. Yes.

GREENWALD. In the Freudian analysis is there such a thing as mental illness?

BIRD. Well, there are disturbed people and adjusted people.

GREENWALD. But *disturbed* and *adjusted* correspond roughly, don't they, to the terms *sick* and *well* as laymen use them?

BIRD. Very roughly, yes.

GREENWALD. Doctor, would you say Commander Queeg suffers from inferiority feelings?

BIRD. Yes, but they are well compensated.

GREENWALD. Is there a difference between *compensated* and *adjusted?*

BIRD. Most definitely.

GREENWALD. Can you explain it?

BIRD. (*Smiles and settles back in his chair.*) Well—let's say a man has some deep-seated psychological disturbance. He can *compensate* by finding outlets for his peculiar drives. He can never *adjust* without undergoing psychoanalysis.

GREENWALD. Has Commander Queeg ever been psychoanalyzed?

BIRD. No.

GREENWALD. He is, then, a disturbed person.

BIRD. Yes, he is. Not disabled however by the disturbance. (*Smiles.*)

GREENWALD. How has he compensated?

BIRD. In two ways, mainly. The paranoid pattern, which is useless and not desirable, and his naval career, which is extremely useful and desirable.

GREENWALD. You say his military career is a result of his disturbance?

BIRD. Most military careers are.

GREENWALD. Doctor, did you note any peculiar habit Commander Queeg had? Something he did with his hands?

BIRD. Do you mean rolling the steel balls?

GREENWALD. Yes, describe the habit, please.

BIRD. Well, it's an incessant rolling or rattling of two marbles in his hand—either hand.

GREENWALD. Why does he do it?

BIRD. His hands tremble. He does it to still his hands and conceal the trembling. It makes him feel more comfortable.

GREENWALD. Why do his hands tremble?

BIRD. The inner tension. It's one of the surface symptoms.

GREENWALD. Does this rolling motion have significance in Freudian analysis?

BIRD. It's an obvious sexual symbol, of course. Now, as to the precise meaning, I—

CHALLEE. (*Rises.*) How far is this totally irrelevant technical discussion going to be pushed?

BLAKELY. (*Scowling*) Are you objecting to the question?

CHALLEE. I'm requesting the court to set limits to time wasting by the defense.

BLAKELY. Your request is noted. Proceed with cross examination.

(CHALLEE *sits.*)

GREENWALD. Doctor, you have testified that the commander is a disturbed, not an adjusted person.

BIRD. Yes.

GREENWALD. He is then in laymen's terms, sick.

BIRD. (*Smiles.*) I remember agreeing to the rough resemblance of the terms *disturbed* and *sick*. But by those terms an awful lot of people are sick—

GREENWALD. But this trial only has Commander Queeg's sickness at issue. If he's sick, how could your board have given him a clean bill of health?

BIRD. You're playing on words, I'm afraid. We found no disability.

GREENWALD. Doctor, supposing the requirements of command were many times as severe as you believe them to be—wouldn't even this mild sickness disable Queeg?

BIRD. That's absurdly hypothetical, because—

GREENWALD. Is it? Have you ever had sea duty, Doctor?

BIRD. No.

GREENWALD. Have you ever *been* to sea?

BIRD. (BIRD *is losing his self-possessed look.*) No.

GREENWALD. How long have you been in the Navy?

BIRD. Five months—no, *six,* I guess, now—

GREENWALD. Have you had any dealings with ships' captains before this case?

BIRD. No.

GREENWALD. On what do you base your estimate of the stresses of command?

BIRD. Well, my general knowledge—

GREENWALD. Do you think command requires a highly gifted, exceptional person?

BIRD. Well, no—

GREENWALD. It doesn't?

BIRD. Not highly gifted, no. Adequate responses, fairly good intelligence, and sufficient training and experience, but—

GREENWALD. Is that enough equipment for, say, a skilled psychiatrist?

BIRD. Well, not exactly—

GREENWALD. In other words, it takes more ability to be a psychiatrist than the captain of a naval vessel?

BIRD. It takes— (*He catches himself, and glances toward* BLAKELY.) That is, different abilities are required. You're making the invidious comparison, not I.

GREENWALD. Doctor, you've admitted Commander Queeg is sick. The only remaining question is, *how* sick. You don't think he's sick enough to be disabled for command. I suggest that since evidently you don't know much about the requirements of command you may be wrong in your conclusion.

BIRD. (*Looking like an insulted boy, his voice quivers.*) I repudiate your suggestion. You've deliberately substituted the word *sick*, which is a loose, a polarized word, for the correct—

GREENWALD. Pardon me, what kind of word?

BIRD. Polarized—loaded, invidious— I never said *sick*. My grasp of the requirements of command is adequate or I would have disqualified myself from serving on the board—

GREENWALD. Maybe you should have.

CHALLEE. (*Rises; shouts.*) The witness is being badgered!

GREENWALD. I withdraw my last statement. No futher questions.

(GREENWALD *strides to his seat.* CHALLEE *crosses to* BIRD *in witness chair.*)

CHALLEE. Doctor Bird, defense counsel managed to put words into your mouth that I'm certain you don't mean, and I'd like to—

BIRD. I'm not aware that he succeeded in putting any words into my mouth.

CHALLEE. (*With an exasperated glance at* GREENWALD) Doctor, he drew the implication from you that Captain Queeg is sick. Surely you don't—

BIRD. Sir, I'm careful in my use of terminology. I did not introduce the term *sick*. I don't regard it as a precise term. Nevertheless, if you're going to use such a loose term, Captain Queeg, like a vast number of seemingly healthy people, is sick. However, he is definitely not disabled for command, which is the only issue here.

CHALLEE. But that sounds like a contradiction, sir, which surely you don't intend—

BIRD. We live in a sick civilization. The well people are exceptional, and Captain Queeg certainly isn't exceptional in that regard, and furthermore—

CHALLEE. (*Hastily, with a worried glance at* BLAKELY.) Thank you, thank you, Doctor, that certainly clarifies the matter. No more questions. (*Goes quickly to his seat.*)

BLAKELY. Doctor— (*Stares at* BIRD *as though considering questioning him, then shrugs.*) Doctor, you will not discuss your testimony outside this courtroom.

BIRD. No, sir.

BLAKELY. Excused.

(*Exit* BIRD.)

CHALLEE. Prosecution rests.

(BLAKELY *glances at wrist watch, then at* GREENWALD, *who comes forward as* CHALLEE *sits.*)

BLAKELY. Is defense ready to present its case?

GREENWALD. Yes, sir.

BLAKELY. How many witnesses are you calling?

GREENWALD. Only two, sir. The first is the accused.

BLAKELY. Then we can button it all up tomorrow morning.

GREENWALD. I believe so, sir.

BLAKELY. (*Rings his bell.*) Recess until 0900.

(COURT *rises.* BLAKELY *goes out.* COURT MEMBERS *follow.* ORDERLY *and* STENOGRAPHER *leave.* CHALLEE *gathers his papers.* GREENWALD *sits slumped in his chair, leaning on one hand, doodling.*)

CHALLEE. (*To* GREENWALD, *when all are gone.*) Quite a job you did on Doctor Bird.

GREENWALD. (*Looks up; in a weary, flat tone*) Thanks, Jack.

CHALLEE. It won't cut any ice.

GREENWALD. No?

CHALLEE. Captain Blakely's headed up a lot of these courts. He doesn't go for vaudeville.

GREENWALD. (*Shrugs.*) See you tomorrow.

CHALLEE. See you tomorrow. (*He goes out.*)

MARYK. Boy, that was marvelous, cutting up that doctor. Wise little bastard.

GREENWALD. (*Strolls to the witness chair and slumps in it.*) Have you ever read it?

MARYK. What?

GREENWALD. Your friend Tom Keefer's novel.

MARYK. Huh?

GREENWALD. *Multitudes, Multitudes.* Have you ever read it?

MARYK. Tom's novel? No, he's always kept it in a black satchel, locked.

GREENWALD. I'd like to read it.

MARYK. You would?

GREENWALD. I'm sure it exposes this war in all its grim futility, and shows up the regular army and navy officers—just a lot of stupid sadists, bitching up the campaigns, and throwing away the lives of fatalistic, humorous, lovable citizen-soldiers. Lots of sexy scenes where the prose becomes rhythmic and beautiful, while the girl gets her pants pulled down.

MARYK. What's eating you?

GREENWALD. I hate this case, do you know? The more so because I want to win it so bad. Because of what I've got to do to win it.

MARYK. I'm beginning to think I've got a chance. You're pretty keen, all right.

GREENWALD. (*Gets up and paces.*) Almost as keen as Mr. Keefer?

MARYK. (*Abashed.*) You were sure right about him. Why did he do it? He didn't have to implicate himself. He could have said what he really thought of Queeg.

GREENWALD. What, to Blakely? Blakely's sniffing around the edges of Keefer as it is. No sir. Your novelist friend's one course was to clam up. He's smart.

MARYK. You don't like Tom much.

GREENWALD. Well, I look at Keefer and I see my own self of a couple of years ago. Only like a crazy-mirror, all distorted and upside down. I'm not amused. Maybe Keefer didn't enjoy sailing under Queeg for half a year. Maybe he'd enjoy it less if the Nazis and the Japs were shaking hands right now at the Mississippi River. I guess what I've found out, Maryk, is that there's a time for everything, including rebellious youth. Possibly you and Mr. Keefer were dead wrong in your timing. In which case the next question is, who's the real victim in this courtroom? You? Or Captain Queeg?

MARYK. Captain Queeg was nuts!

GREENWALD. You heard Dr. Lundeen. It's a question of degree. If you're in a war and your command personnel is stretched thin, maybe you've got to use him because he's got the training. I think Captain Queeg was a mean, stupid son of a bitch, but—

MARYK. Okay!

GREENWALD. Maryk, if that was grounds for deposing your superior officer we wouldn't have an army or a navy. That's a widespread opinion of superior officers.

MARYK. They're not all Queegs.

GREENWALD. Superiors all tend to look like Queeg from underneath. It's an unflattering angle.

MARYK. What do you do when you really get a Queeg?

GREENWALD. You fight the war. Where can we get drunk? I mean drunk.

MARYK. Mister, you've got a day's work to do in court tomorrow.

GREENWALD. I know exactly what I've got to do in court tomorrow. That's why I want to get drunk. Come on, let's
go.

(*They go out.*)

STAGE LIGHTS FADE.

HOUSE LIGHTS COME ON.

ACT TWO

SCENE I

The Defense

THE SCENE: *House LIGHTS dim. The LIGHTS brighten on an empty stage, the setting unchanged from the end of Act One. Enter* ORDERLY, STENOGRAPHER, GREENWALD, MARYK, CHALLEE, *and the six* COURT MEMBERS. ALL *take their places, standing.*

CHALLEE. Attention!

BLAKELY. (*Enters; takes his seat. Rings bell.*) Defense, present your case.

(ALL *sit except* GREENWALD.)

GREENWALD. I call the accused.

(MARYK *stands.*)

BLAKELY. Does the accused request that he be permitted to testify?

MARYK. I do so request, sir.

BLAKELY. You have the right to do so. You also have the right not to take the stand. If you don't take the stand that fact won't be to your prejudice. If you take the stand you may be subjected to a rigorous cross-examination.

MARYK. I understand that, sir.

BLAKELY. Court stenographer will affirmatively record that the statutory request was made.
(MARYK *takes stand. Bible business.*)
You do solemnly swear that the evidence you shall give in this court shall be the truth, the whole truth, and nothing but the truth. So help you God.

MARYK. I do. (*Takes witness stand.*)

GREENWALD. State your name, rank, and present station.

MARYK. Stephen Maryk, Lieutenant U.S.N.R., executive officer of the U.S.S. *Caine*.

GREENWALD. Are you the accused in this court-martial?

MARYK. I am.

GREENWALD. What was your occupation in civilian life?

MARYK. Helping out in my father's fishing business. We own a couple of boats.

GREENWALD. Where?

MARYK. Here in San Francisco.

GREENWALD. Then you were familiar with the problems of ocean-going ship-handling before entering the Navy?

MARYK. Well, I've been on the boats since I was fourteen.

GREENWALD. Did you relieve the commanding officer of the *Caine* of his command on December 18, 1944?

MARYK. I did.

GREENWALD. Was the *Caine* in the last extremity when you relieved the captain?

MARYK. It was.

GREENWALD. On what facts do you base that judgment?

MARYK. (*Runs his tongue over his lips.*) Well, several things, like—well, we were unable to hold course. We broached to three times in an hour.

GREENWALD. Broached to.

MARYK. Yes. Wind and sea took charge and tossed us sideways for ten minutes at a time. We were rolling too steeply for the inclinometer to record. We were shipping solid green water in the wheelhouse. The generators were cutting out. The ship wasn't answering to emergency rudder and engine settings. We were lost and out of control.

GREENWALD. Did you point these things out to the captain?

MARYK. Repeatedly for an hour. I begged him to come north and head into the wind.

GREENWALD. What was his response?

MARYK. Well, mostly a glazed look and no answer, or a repetition of his own desires.

GREENWALD. Which were what?

MARYK. I guess to hold fleet course until we went down.

GREENWALD. Mister Maryk, when did you start keeping your medical log on Captain Queeg?

MARYK. Shortly after the Kwajalein invasion.

GREENWALD. Why did you start it?

MARYK. Well, I began to think the captain might be mentally ill.

GREENWALD. Why?

MARYK. That yellow dye marker business.

GREENWALD. Was that the incident in which Captain Queeg acquired the nickname "Old Yellowstain"?

MARYK. Yes, it was.

GREENWALD. You witnessed the occurrence yourself?

MARYK. I was navigator. I was right there on the bridge.

GREENWALD. Describe the Yellowstain incident, please.

MARYK. Well, it was the first morning of the invasion. We were ordered to lead a group of attack boats in to the beach. That is, we had to take them to their line of departure, one thousand yards from the beach. These little boats lay so low in the water they couldn't see to navigate for themselves. They needed a guide to make sure they hit the right island and the right beach. Captain Queeg rang up ten knots and we started to head in toward this island. It had some funny Jap name. Our code name for it was Jacob Island. Well, it was a choppy sea. These assault boats could only make five or six knots. And at that they were shipping solid water, and the marines were getting just about drowned in spray. They began to fall way behind. Naturally they signalled for us to slow down. But the captain just ignored them. We pulled further and further ahead until we could hardly see them. Then, when we were about twenty-five hundred yards from the beach, we heard some gunfire. The captain suddenly yelled, "We're running up on the beach! Reverse course! Make thirty knots!" And while we were turning he threw over one of these yellow dye markers you use to mark water where there's a floating mine or something. So we went barrelling out of there. The attack boats were just a lot of specks way off in the distance. All you could see behind us was this big spread of yellow, all over the water.

(*A long pause.*)

GREENWALD. Now, Mister Maryk—

BLAKELY. (*Rings his bell.*) Court wants to question the witness. Lieutenant, how do you know you were twenty-five hundred yards from the beach when you turned?

MARYK. Sir, I was navigating. There wasn't a doubt in the world where we were, by visual plot. And our radar range to the beach was also twenty-five hundred when we turned.

BLAKELY. Did you inform your captain that he was turning fifteen hundred yards short?

MARYK. Sir, I shouted it at him, over and over. He just stood there smiling.

BLAKELY. (*Making notes*) You say these boats signalled to you to slow down.

MARYK. Yes, sir. By semaphore.

BLAKELY. Was the signal reported to your captain?

MARYK. I reported it myself.

BLAKELY. Was he aware of the fact that you were running away from the boats?

MARYK. He was looking right at them, sir. I pointed out that if we got too far ahead, the boats wouldn't know where the line of departure was. That's when he said, "Well, we'll throw over a dye marker, then."

(BLAKELY *nods to* GREENWALD.)

GREENWALD. Mister Maryk, why didn't you go to higher authority at once with your doubts about the captain's mental health?

MARYK. I figured if I only had a record I'd be on stronger ground. So I decided to start the log. I figured if ever I was all wrong I'd just burn it. I kept it under lock and key.

GREENWALD. What, in your view, made an incident worthy of record in your medical log?

MARYK. Just any act that seemed strange or abnormal. Like the Silex business.

GREENWALD. Describe the Silex business.

MARYK. A mess boy slopped coffee on a Silex and burned it out. None of the mess boys would admit which one did it. So the captain ordered all the officers of the ship to sit as a court of inquiry till we found out who burned out the Silex. I mean in itself it's a silly little thing. But it went on and on for thirty-six hours. All ship's work stopped. There we were, all of us in the wardroom, dying for sleep, needing shaves, and still trying to find out which of those poor colored boys burned out the Silex. By then those kids thought whoever did it was going to get hung. They would have died before telling us. So finally I had to go to the captain and tell him that all the officers admitted they were incompetent investigators and would take cuts in their fitness reports, but they couldn't find out who slopped coffee on the Silex. So, he made a note in his black book and called off the inquiry. Things like that. Or like the water business.

GREENWALD. Describe water business.

MARYK. It's all in the log. How he cut off the water at the equator for two days for the whole ship. Just because he caught one simple deckhand stealing a drink during water conservation hours. Or plain crazy things, like the strawberry business.

GREENWALD. Describe the strawberry business.

MARYK. Well, there—

CHALLEE. (*Rises.*) Objection. The so-called medical log was introduced in evidence at the start of these proceedings. All this is just repeating a lot of trivial disloyal gripes.

GREENWALD. If the court concurs, I'll pass over the medical log.

(CHALLEE *sits.*)

BLAKELY. (*With a glance around at the* COURT MEMBERS, *uneasily*) Well, let's not take up time here.

GREENWALD. Aye aye, sir.

BLAKELY. Only—there seems to be some confusion about the so-called strawberry business. It started out as a search for a quart of strawberries, didn't it?

MARYK. Yes, sir.

BLAKELY. Then it somehow became a search for a key.

MARYK. That's right.

BLAKELY. How was that?

MARYK. That was on account of the cheese business.

BLAKELY. Cheese business? I don't recall any cheese business.

MARYK. That was on the first ship Captain Queeg served on, sir, when he was an ensign. Cheese had been disappearing from ship's stores. He investigated and caught a sailor who had made himself a duplicate key to a padlock on the refrigerator. Well, for catching this cheese thief the captain had gotten a letter of commendation. This was peace time. Naturally, he was real proud of it. When this strawberry thing came up he insisted it was the same thing, and all we had to do was find out who had made a duplicate key to the wardroom icebox. But of course it was ridiculous. It was the mess boys again. We all knew they'd eaten up this quart of strawberries. It was just the leavings from the wardroom mess, and they were entitled to eat it, that was the custom. But naturally when the captain started to roar around about "those strawberries," why, the boys just froze up and swore they hadn't eaten them. And the captain, he was so steamed up on this key theory, he believed them.

BLAKELY. So he ordered the search for the key?

MARYK. Yes, sir. We never saw Captain Queeg so happy before or since. He was living the cheese business all over
again. He organized the search himself. All ship's work
was suspended. We collected every single key on the ship
—boxes of keys, barrels of keys, about twenty-eight hundred of them all tagged with the owner's name. Then to
make sure we had them all we searched the ship from
stem to stern, from the crow's nest to the bilge. We
stripped the crew stark naked, every one of them, shook
out their clothes. We searched their lockers. We crawled
into every hole and every space in the ship. We crawled
under the boilers and pulled out the lead ballast blocks,
two hundred pounds apiece. This went on for three days,
and all of it over a key that never existed. Well, when I
saw Captain Queeg sitting by the icebox, taking those
keys one by one out of the barrels and trying them on the
padlock, hours on end, with a gleam in his eye, I gave up.
That was when I showed the medical log to Lieutenant
Keefer.

BLAKELY. Mister Maryk, when Lieutenant Keefer finished
reading your medical log, what was his first comment?

(*All six* COURT MEMBERS *stare intently at* MARYK.)

MARYK. (*Pause.*) Sir, I'm afraid I don't remember.

BLAKELY. Did he encourage you to go to Admiral Halsey?

MARYK. I did that on my own responsibility, sir.

BLAKELY. But he went with you to the *New Jersey*.

MARYK. He did, sir.

BLAKELY. So at first—he didn't discourage you?

MARYK. Well, sir, when we got aboard the *New Jersey* he
discouraged me. He said we shouldn't go through with it.
And we didn't.

BLAKELY. Would you say his testimony on the subject was
substantially correct?

MARYK. Yes, sir. It was all my doing, sir.

(BLAKELY *nods to* GREENWALD.)

GREENWALD. (*Rises.*) Mister Maryk, when the typhoon was over, did Captain Queeg make any effort to regain command?

MARYK. Yes, on the morning of the nineteenth. The storm had blown out. We'd just sighted the fleet.

GREENWALD. Describe what happened.

MARYK. Well, I was in the charthouse writing up a despatch to report the relief to Admiral Halsey. The captain came in and said, "Do you mind coming to my cabin and having a talk before you send that?" I went below and we talked. It was the same thing—at first, about how I'd be court-martialled for mutiny. He said, "You've applied for transfer to the regular navy. You know this means the end of all that, don't you?" Then he went into a long thing about how he loved the Navy and had no other interest in life, and even if he was cleared this would ruin his record. I said I felt sorry for him, and I really did. Finally he came out with his proposal. He said he'd forget the whole thing and never report me. He would resume command, and the whole matter would be forgotten and written off—

GREENWALD. What did you say to the proposal?

MARYK. Well, I was amazed. I said, "Captain, the whole ship knows about it. It's written up in the quartermaster's log and the O.O.D.'s log." Well, he hemmed and hawed, and finally said it wouldn't be the first time a pencilled rough log had been corrected and fixed up after the fact.

GREENWALD. Did you remind him of the rule against erasures?

MARYK. Yes, and he kind of laughed and said it was either that or a court-martial for mutiny for me, and a black mark on his record which he didn't deserve. He didn't see that a few penciled rough lines were worth all that.

GREENWALD. What followed?

MARYK. Well he began to plead and beg—he cried at one point—in the end he became terrifically angry, and ordered me out of his cabin. So I sent the despatch.

GREENWALD. Then you had the chance, twenty-four hours later, of expunging the whole event from the official record with the captain's knowledge and approval?

MARYK. Yes.

GREENWALD. Mister Maryk, were you panicky at all during the typhoon?

MARYK. I was not.

GREENWALD. Now, Lieutenant, you're charged with relieving your captain willfully, without authority, and without justifiable cause. Did you relieve Captain Queeg willfully?

MARYK. Yes, I knew what I was doing.

GREENWALD. Did you relieve without authority?

MARYK. No. My authority was Articles 184, 185, 186.

GREENWALD. Did you relieve without justifiable cause?

MARYK. No. My justifiable cause was the captain's mental breakdown at a time when the ship was in danger.

GREENWALD. No further questions. (*Sits.*)

CHALLEE. (*Approaches* MARYK.) Mister Maryk, this amazing interview in which the captain offered to falsify official records. Were there any witnesses to it?

MARYK. We were alone in the captain's cabin. No.

CHALLEE. This incident at Kwajalein. Did anyone else see this chart which, according to you, indicated your ship turned away from the beach too soon?

MARYK. About an hour after it happened the captain asked to see the chart and took it to his cabin. When I got it back all my bearings and course lines had been erased.

CHALLEE. Then you have no documentary corroboration of this story.

MARYK. No.

CHALLEE. How about the radar men who called off the ranges? Won't they confirm your story?

MARYK. Sir, you can't expect them to remember one single radar range, when they called them by the thousands in every invasion.

CHALLEE. These poor abandoned marines in the assault boats never complained to higher authority of the dastardly conduct of the *Caine?*

MARYK. No.

CHALLEE. Strange.

MARYK. Sir, they landed against machine gun fire. The ones that survived, I don't think they remembered much else besides that landing.

CHALLEE. Mister Maryk, who coined this scurrilous nickname, "Old Yellowstain"?

MARYK. (*A worried look at* GREENWALD.) Well, it just sprang into existence.

CHALLEE. Throughout the ship? Or just among the officers?

MARYK. Among the officers.

CHALLEE. You're sure you didn't coin it yourself?

MARYK. I didn't.

CHALLEE. Mister Maryk, what kind of rating would you give yourself for loyalty to your captain?

MARYK. I think I was a loyal officer.

CHALLEE. Did you issue a seventy-two hour pass to Stilwell in December '43 against the captain's express instructions?

MARYK. I did.

CHALLEE. Do you call that a loyal act?

MARYK. No.

CHALLEE. You admit to a disloyal act in your first days as executive officer?

MARYK. Yes.

CHALLEE. Mister Maryk—where did you get your schooling?

MARYK. Public schools, San Francisco. And San Francisco University.

CHALLEE. How were your grades in elementary school?

MARYK. Okay.

CHALLEE. Average? Above average? Below average?

MARYK. Average.

CHALLEE. How about your high school grades?

MARYK. Well, I didn't do so good there. Below average.

CHALLEE. What kind of course did you take at college?

MARYK. Business course.

CHALLEE. Any pre-medical courses?

MARYK. No.

CHALLEE. Any psychology or psychiatry courses?

MARYK. No.

CHALLEE. How were your grades at college?

MARYK. I scraped by.

CHALLEE. Below average?

MARYK. Yes.

CHALLEE. Where did you get all of these high-falutin' ideas about paranoia?

MARYK. (*With a worried glance toward* GREENWALD) I—out of books.

CHALLEE. What books? Name the titles.

MARYK. Medical-type books about mental illness.

CHALLEE. Oh, was that your intellectual hobby—reading about psychiatry?

MARYK. No.

CHALLEE. Then where did you get these books?

MARYK. I—borrowed them off ships' doctors here and there.

CHALLEE. And with your background, your scholastic record —did you imagine you understood these highly technical, scientific works?

MARYK. Well, I got something out of them.

CHALLEE. What is a conditioned reflex?

MARYK. I don't know.

CHALLEE. What is schizophrenia?

MARYK. I think it's a mental illness.

CHALLEE. You think so. What are its symptoms?

MARYK. I don't know.

CHALLEE. In fact, you don't know what you're talking about when you discuss mental illness, is that right?

MARYK. I didn't say I knew much about it.

CHALLEE. Have you ever heard the expression, "A little learning is a dangerous thing"?

MARYK. Yes.

CHALLEE. You got a headful of terms you didn't understand, and on that basis you had the temerity to depose a commanding officer on the grounds of mental illness. Is that correct?

MARYK. I didn't relieve him because of what the books said. The ship was in danger—

CHALLEE. Never mind the ship. We're discussing your grasp of psychiatry. Have you heard the diagnosis of the qualified psychiatrists who examined your captain?

MARYK. Yes.

CHALLEE. What was their diagnosis—was he crazy or wasn't he, on 18 December?

MARYK. They say he wasn't.

CHALLEE. But, you, with your whining gripes about strawberries and Silexes, know better. Mister Maryk, who was the third ranking officer on your ship?

MARYK. Lieutenant Keefer.

CHALLEE. Was he a good officer?

MARYK. Yes.

CHALLEE. Do you consider his mind as good as yours? Or perhaps better?

MARYK. Better.

CHALLEE. You showed this medical log of yours to him?

MARYK. Yes.

CHALLEE He wasn't convinced by it that the captain was mentally ill.

MARYK. No.

CHALLEE. He talked you out of trying to have the captain relieved.

MARYK. Yes.

CHALLEE. And yet two weeks later—despite the whole weight of naval discipline—despite the arguments of the next officer in rank to you, a superior intellect—despite all this, you went ahead and seized command of your ship?

MARYK. I relieved him because he definitely seemed sick during the typhoon.

CHALLEE. You *still* imagine your diagnosis of Captain Queeg is superior to the doctor's?

MARYK. Only about Queeg on the morning of the typhoon.

CHALLEE. No more questions. (*Sits.*)

GREENWALD. (*Rises.*) No re-examination.

BLAKELY. You may step down, Lieutenant.

(MARYK *leaves the stand with a stunned expression and goes to his seat.* BLAKELY *glances at* GREENWALD.)

GREENWALD. Call Lieutenant Commander Queeg.

(*Exit* ORDERLY. *Returns with* QUEEG, *who looks as debonair and assured as on the first day. He hesitates before taking witness chair, expecting to be sworn.*)

BLAKELY. Commander, the oath previously taken by you is still binding.

QUEEG. Yes, sir.

(QUEEG *takes witness chair.* GREENWALD *approaches* QUEEG.)

GREENWALD. Commander, on the morning of 19 December, did you have an interview in your room with Lieutenant Maryk?

QUEEG. Let's see. That's the day after the typhoon. Yes, I did.

GREENWALD. Was it at your request?

QUEEG. Yes.

GREENWALD. What was the substance of that interview?

QUEEG. Well, as I say, I felt sorry for him. I hated to see him ruining his life with one panicky mistake. Particularly as I knew his ambition was to make the Navy his career. I tried as hard as I could to show him what a mistake he had made. I recommended that he relinquish command to me, and I offered to be as lenient as I could in reporting what had happened.

GREENWALD. You never offered not to report the incident?

QUEEG. How could I? It was already recorded in the logs.

GREENWALD. Were the logs in pencil, or typed, or what?

QUEEG. That would make no difference.

GREENWALD. Were they in pencil, Commander?

QUEEG. Well, let's see. Probably they were—quartermaster log and O.O.D. rough log always are. I doubt the yeoman would have gotten around to typing smooth logs in all the excitement.

GREENWALD. Did you offer to erase the incident from the pencilled logs and make no report at all?

QUEEG. I did not. Erasures aren't permitted in pencilled logs.

GREENWALD. Lieutenant Maryk has testified under oath, Commander, that you made such an offer. Not only that, but you begged and pleaded and even wept to get him to agree to erase those few pencil lines, in return for which you promised to hush up the incident completely and make no report.

QUEEG. (*Calmly and pleasantly*) That isn't true.

GREENWALD. There isn't any truth in it at all?

QUEEG. Well, it's a distortion of what I told you. My version is the exact truth.

GREENWALD. You deny the proposal to erase the logs and hush up the story?

QUEEG. I deny it completely. That's the part he made up— And the weeping and the pleading. That's fantastic.

GREENWALD. You are accusing Mister Maryk of perjury?

QUEEG. I'm not accusing him. He's accused of enough as it stands. You're likely to hear a lot of strange things from Mister Maryk about me, that's all.

GREENWALD. Isn't one of you obviously not telling the truth about that interview?

QUEEG. It appears so.

GREENWALD. Can you prove it isn't you?

QUEEG. Only by citing a clean record of over fourteen years as a naval officer, against the word of a man on trial for a mutinous act.

GREENWALD. Commander, did you ever receive a hundred ten dollars from Lieutenant Junior Grade Keith?

QUEEG. I don't recall offhand that I did.

GREENWALD. He testified that you did.

QUEEG. I did? On what occasion?

GREENWALD. On the occasion of a loss of a crate of yours in San Francisco Bay.

QUEEG. Yes. I remember now. It was over a year ago. December or thereabouts. He was responsible for the loss and insisted on paying, and so he did.

GREENWALD. What was in the crate, Commander, that cost a hundred and ten dollars?

QUEEG. Oh, uniforms, books, navigating instruments—the usual.

GREENWALD. How was Keith responsible for the loss?

QUEEG. Well, he was boat officer and in charge of the loading. He issued foolish and contradictory orders. The men got rattled and the crate fell into the water and sank.

GREENWALD. A wooden crate full of clothes sank?

QUEEG. There were other things in it, I guess. I had some souvenir coral rocks.

GREENWALD. Commander, wasn't the crate entirely full of bottles of intoxicating liquor?

QUEEG. (*After a barely perceptible pause*) Certainly not.

GREENWALD. Keith has testified you charged him for a crate of liquor.

QUEEG. You'll hear plenty of strange distortions about me from Keith and Maryk. They're the two culprits here and they're apt to make all kinds of strange statements.

GREENWALD. Did you make this crate yourself?

QUEEG. No. My carpenter's mate did.

GREENWALD. What was his name?

QUEEG. I don't recall. It'll be on the personnel records. He's been gone from the ship a long time.

GREENWALD. Where is this carpenter's mate now, Commander?

QUEEG. I don't know. I transferred him to the beach at Funafuti at the request of the commodore for a carpenter. This was back in May.

GREENWALD. You don't recall his name?

QUEEG. No.

GREENWALD. Was it Carpenter's Mate Second Class Otis F. Langhorne?

QUEEG. Lang, Langhorne. Sounds right.

GREENWALD. Commander, there is a Carpenter's Mate First Class Otis F. Langhorne at present in damage-control school at Treasure Island, right here in the bay. Defense has arranged to subpoena him if necessary.

QUEEG. (*Shoots a look at* CHALLEE.) You're sure it's the same one?

GREENWALD. His service record shows twenty-one months aboard the *Caine*. Your signature is in it. Would it be useful to have him subpoenaed, sir?

CHALLEE. (*Rises.*) Objection to this entire irrelevancy about the crate, and request it be stricken from the record.

GREENWALD. The credibility of the witness is being established. I submit to the court that nothing could be more relevant to this trial.

BLAKELY. Overruled. (*Nods to* STENOGRAPHER.)

(CHALLEE *sits.*)

STENOGRAPHER. (*Reads.*) "Would it be useful to have him subpoenaed, sir?"

QUEEG. Well, it's a question which crate Langhorne nailed up. I had two crates, as I recall now.

GREENWALD. Oh?
(*Pause.*)
Well. This is a new angle, not mentioned by Keith. Did Langhorne make both crates, sir?

QUEEG. Well, I don't recall whether I had both crates on that occasion or two crates on two different occasions. It's all very trivial and happened a long time ago and I've had a year of combat steaming in between and a typhoon and all this hospital business and I'm not too clear.

GREENWALD. Commander, there are many points in this trial which turn on the issue of credibility between yourself and other officers. If you wish I will request a five-minute recess while you clear your mind as well as you can on the matter of these crates.

QUEEG. That won't be necessary. Just let me think for a moment, please.

(*In the silence* BLAKELY's *pencil makes a thin, rattling noise as he rolls it under his palm on the bench.* QUEEG *sits staring from under his eyebrows.*)

Kay. I have it straight now. I made a misstatement. I lost a crate in San Diego Harbor back in '38 or '39 I think it was, under similar circumstances. That was the one containing clothes. The crate Keith lost did contain liquor.

GREENWALD. Was it entirely full of liquor?

QUEEG. I believe it was—

GREENWALD. How did you obtain a crate full of whiskey, Commander, in wartime?

QUEEG. Bought up the rations of my officers at the wine mess in Pearl.

GREENWALD. You transported this liquor from Pearl to the States in your ship? Do you know the regulations—

QUEEG. (*Breaks in.*) I'm aware of regulations. The crate was sealed prior to getting under way. I gave it the same locked stowage I gave the medicinal brandy. Liquor was damned scarce and expensive in the States. I'd had three years of steady combat duty. I gave myself this leeway as captain of the *Caine* and it was a common practice and I believe rank has its privileges, as they say. I had no intentions of concealing it from the court and I'm not ashamed of it. I simply mixed up the two crates in my mind.

GREENWALD. Keith testified, Commander, that you gave all the orders to the boat crew which caused the loss of the crate.

QUEEG. That's a lie.

GREENWALD. Also that you refused to sign his leave papers until he paid for the loss.

QUEEG. That's another lie.

GREENWALD. It seems to be the issue of credibility again, sir —this time your word against Keith's. Correct?

QUEEG. You'll hear nothing but lies about me from Keith. He has an insane hatred of me.

GREENWALD. Do you know why, sir?

QUEEG. I can't say, unless it's his resentment against fancied injuries to his crony, this sailor Stilwell. Those two were mighty affectionate.

GREENWALD. Affectionate, sir?

QUEEG. Well, it seems to me every time Keith thought I looked crosseyed at Stilwell there was all kinds of screeching and hollering from Keith as though I were picking on his wife or something. And those two sure ganged up mighty fast to back Maryk when he relieved me.

GREENWALD. Commander, are you suggesting there were abnormal relations between Lieutenant Keith and the sailor Stilwell?

QUEEG. I'm not suggesting a thing. I'm stating plain facts that everybody knew who had eyes to see.

GREENWALD. (Looking around at BLAKELY) Does the court desire to caution the witness about the gravity of the insinuated charge?

QUEEG. (Nasally) I'm not insinuating a thing, sir! I don't know of anything improper between those two men and I deny insinuating anything. All I said Keith was always taking Stilwell's part and it's the easiest thing in the world to prove and that's all I said or meant. I resent the twisting of my words.

BLAKELY. Are you going to pursue this—topic?

GREENWALD. No, sir.

BLAKELY. Very well. Go ahead.

GREENWALD. Commander, during the period when the *Caine* was towing targets at Pearl Harbor did you ever steam over your own towline and cut it?

CHALLEE. (*Stands.*) Objection! This towline business is the last straw. The tactics of the defense counsel are an outrage on the dignity of these proceedings. He's systematically turning this trial into a court-martial of Commander Queeg.

GREENWALD. Sir, the judge advocate has made it perfectly clear that he thinks he has a prima facie case in the report of the two psychiatrists. But I say it's still up to the court, not to shore-bound doctors, however brilliant, to decide whether the captain of the *Caine* was mentally well enough to retain his self-control and his post during a typhoon.

BLAKELY. The objection is overruled. The witness will answer the question. (*Nods to* STENOGRAPHER.)

STENOGRAPHER. (*Reads.*) "Commander Queeg, during the period when the *Caine* was towing targets at Pearl Harbor did you ever steam over your own towline and cut it?"

QUEEG. (*Promptly*) Kay, now—here's the story on that particular slander. I started to make a turn, when I noticed some anti-aircraft bursts close aboard to starboard. I was gravely concerned that my ship might be within range of somebody's firing. We were in a gunnery area. I was watching the bursts. This same sailor Stilwell, a very dreamy and unreliable man, was at the helm. He failed to warn me that we were coming around the full three hundred and sixty degrees. I saw what was happening, finally, and instantly reversed course, and I avoided passing over the towline, to my best knowledge. However, the line parted during the turn.

GREENWALD. You say you were distracted by AA bursts. Did anything else distract you?

QUEEG. Not that I recall.

GREENWALD. Were you engaged in reprimanding a signalman named Urban at length for having his shirttail out, while your ship was turning three hundred sixty degrees?

QUEEG. Who says that—Keith again?

GREENWALD. Will you answer the question, Commander?

QUEEG. It's a malicious lie, of course.

GREENWALD. Was Urban on the bridge at the time?

QUEEG. Yes.

GREENWALD. Was his shirttail out?

QUEEG. Yes, and I reprimanded him. That took me about two seconds. I'm not in the habit of dwelling on those things. Then there were those AA bursts, and that was what distracted me.

GREENWALD. Did you point out these AA bursts to the officer of the deck or the exec?

QUEEG. I may have. I don't recall. I didn't run weeping to my O.O.D. on every occasion. I may very well have kept my own counsel. And since this shirttail thing has been brought up—I'd like to say that Ensign Keith as morale officer was in charge of enforcing uniform regulations and completely soldiered on the job. When I took over the ship it was like the Chinese Navy. And I bore down on Keith to watch those shirttails and for all I know that's another reason he hated me and circulated all this about my cutting the towline.

GREENWALD. Did you drop a yellow dye marker off Jacob Island on the first morning of the invasion of Kwajalein?

QUEEG. I may have. I don't recall.

GREENWALD. Do you recall what your first mission was during the invasion?

QUEEG. To lead a group of attack boats to the line of departure for Jacob Island.

GREENWALD. Did you fulfill that mission?

QUEEG. Yes.

GREENWALD. Why did you drop the dye marker?

QUEEG. I don't know for sure that I did drop one. Maybe I dropped one to mark the line of departure plainly.

GREENWALD. How far was the line of departure from the beach?

QUEEG. As I recall, a thousand yards.

GREENWALD. Commander, didn't you run a mile ahead of the attack boats, drop your dye marker more than half a mile short, and retire at high speed, leaving the boats to grope their way to the line of departure as best they could?

CHALLEE. (Rises.) The question is abusive and flagrantly leading.

GREENWALD. (Wearily) I am willing to withdraw the question, in view of the commander's dim memory, and proceed to more recent events.

BLAKELY. Court desires to question the witness.

(GREENWALD *crosses to his desk. Sits.*)

Commander Queeg, in view of the implications in this line of testimony, I urge you to search your memory for correct answers.

QUEEG. I am certainly trying to do that, sir, but these are very small points. I've been through several campaigns since Kwajalein and the typhoon and now all this business—

BLAKELY. I appreciate that. It will facilitate justice if you can remember enough to give a few definite answers on points of fact. First of all, were those boats on the line of departure when you turned away from the beach?

QUEEG. As near as I could calculate, yes.

BLAKELY. In that case, Commander, if they were already on the line, what purpose did the dye marker serve?

QUEEG. (*Hesitates.*) Well, you might say a safety factor. Just another added mark. Now—maybe I erred in being overcautious and making sure they knew where they were but then again, sir, I've always believed you can't err on the side of safety.

BLAKELY. (*Slight acrid impatience.*) Did you have the conn?

QUEEG. (*Pauses.*) As I recall now Lieutenant Maryk had the conn, and I now recall I had to caution him for opening the gap too wide between us and the boats.

BLAKELY. How wide?

QUEEG. I can't say, but at one point there was definitely too much open water and I called him aside and I admonished him not to run away from the boats.

BLAKELY. Didn't you direct him to slow down when you saw the gap widening?

QUEEG. Well, but it was all happening very fast and I may have been watching the beach for a few seconds and then I saw we were running away. And so that's why I dropped the marker, to compensate for Maryk's running away from the boats.

BLAKELY. (*Pauses; face grave.*) These are your factual recollections, Commander?

QUEEG. Those are the facts, sir.

BLAKELY. (*To* GREENWALD.) Resume your examination.

GREENWALD. (*Leaning against his desk, speaks at once.*) Commander Queeg, did you make it a practice, during invasions, to station yourself on the side of the bridge that was sheltered from the beach?

QUEEG. (*Angrily*) That's an insulting question, and the answer is no. I had to be on all sides of the bridge at once, constantly moving from one side to the other because Maryk was navigator and Keith was my O.O.D. at general quarters and both of them were invariably scurrying to the safe side of the bridge so I was captain and navigator and O.O.D. all rolled in one and that's why I had to move constantly from one side of the bridge to the other. And that's the truth, whatever lies may have been said about me in this court. (*Takes two silvery steel balls out of his pocket.*)

BLAKELY. (*Rings bell.*) The court will question the witness.

(GREENWALD *sits.*)

CHALLEE. (*Stands.*) Sir, the witness is obviously and understandably agitated by this ordeal, and I request a recess to give him a breathing space—

QUEEG. I am not in the least agitated, and I'm glad to answer any and all questions here and in fact I demand a chance to set the record straight on anything derogatory to me in the testimony that's gone before. I did not make a single mistake in fifteen months aboard the *Caine* and I can prove it and my record has been spotless until now and I don't want it smirched by a whole lot of lies and distortions by disloyal officers.

BLAKELY. Commander, would you like a recess?

QUEEG. Definitely not, sir. I request there be no recess if it's up to me.

BLAKELY. Very well. I simply want to ask—if the performance of these two officers was so unspeakably bad, why did you tolerate it? Why didn't you beach them? Or at least rotate them to less responsible battle stations?

QUEEG. Well sir, strange as it may seem, the fact is I am a very soft-hearted guy. Not many people know that. I never despaired of training those two men up and making naval officers of them. I kept them under my eye just because I wanted to train them up. The last thing I wanted to do was wreck their careers. Not that they had any similar concern for me, either of them.

BLAKELY. Defense counsel!

GREENWALD. (*Rises.*) Commander, on the morning of 18 December, at the moment you were relieved, was the *Caine* in the last extremity?

QUEEG. It certainly was not!

GREENWALD. Was it in grave danger at that moment?

QUEEG. Absolutely not. I had that ship under complete control. (*Puts steel balls away.*)

GREENWALD. Did you ever indicate to your other officers that it had been your intention to change course and come north at ten o'clock or fifteen minutes after Maryk did?

QUEEG. (*Pause.*) Yes, I did make that statement, and such had been my intention.

GREENWALD. Why did you intend to abandon fleet course, Commander, if the ship wasn't in danger?

QUEEG. (*After a long silence.*) Well, I don't see any inconsistency there. I've repeatedly stated in my testimony that my rule is safety first. As I say the ship wasn't in danger but a typhoon is still a typhoon and I'd just about decided that we'd do as well coming around to north. I might have executed my intention at ten o'clock and then again I might not have.

GREENWALD. Then Maryk's decision to come north was not a panicky, irrational blunder?

QUEEG. His panicky blunder was relieving me. I kept *him* from making any disastrous mistakes thereafter. I didn't intend to vindicate myself at the cost of all the lives on the *Caine*.

GREENWALD. Commander Queeg, have you read Lieutenant Maryk's medical log?

QUEEG. Oh, yes, I have read that interesting document, yes, sir, I have. It is the biggest conglomeration of lies and distortions and half-truths I've ever seen and I'm extremely glad you asked me because I want to get my side of it all on the record.

GREENWALD. Please state your version, or any factual comments on the episodes in the log, sir.

QUEEG. Kay. Now, starting right with that strawberry business the real truth is that I was betrayed and thrown and double-crossed by my executive officer and this precious gentleman Mister Keith who between them corrupted my wardroom so that I was one man against a whole ship without any support from my officers.—Kay. Now, you take that strawberry business—why, if that wasn't a case of outright conspiracy to protect a malefactor from justice —Maryk carefully leaves out the little fact that I had conclusively proved by a process of elimination that someone had a key to the icebox. He says it was the steward's mates who ate the strawberries but if I wanted to take the trouble I could prove to this court geometrically that they couldn't have. It's the water business all over again, like when the crew was taking baths seven times a day and our evaps were definitely on the fritz half the time and I was trying to inculcate the simplest principles of water conservation, but no, Mister Maryk the hero of the crew wanted to go right on mollycoddling them and— Or you take the coffee business—No! Well, the strawberry thing first—it all hinged on a thorough search for the key and that was where Mister Maryk as usual with the help of Mister Keith fudged it. Just went through a lot of phony motions that proved nothing and— Like thinking the incessant burning out of Silexes which were government property was a joke, which was the attitude of everybody from Maryk down, no sense of responsibility though I emphasized over and over that the war wouldn't last forever, that all these things would have to be accounted for. It was a constant battle, always the same thing, Maryk and Keith undermining my authority, always arguments, though I personally liked Keith and kept trying to train him up only to get stabbed in the back when— Kay, I think I've covered the strawberry business and— Oh, yes, this mess account business. I had to watch them like a hawk. And believe me I did. They didn't sneak any fast one by but it wasn't for not trying. Instead of paying some attention to their accounts and their inventories which I had to check over and over, always a few pennies short or a few dollars over—what did it matter to them, keeping accurate records? Let the captain worry. And I did, by God. I defy anyone to check over a single wardroom mess statement or ship's service inventory filed aboard the U.S.S. *Caine* while I was captain and find a mistake of one single solitary cent, and I mean I defy a certified public accountant to do it. Kay, what else? There was so much tripe in that precious log of Mister Maryk's— Oh, yes, the movie business. Kay. No respect for command was the whole trouble with that ship, and the movie operator, who had a disrespectful surly manner anyway, blithely started the movie without waiting for the arrival of the commanding officer. And out of that whole ship's crew, officers and men, did one person call a halt or even notice that the captain wasn't present? I missed those movies more than they did, but I banned them and by God I'd do it again. What was I supposed to do, issue letters of commendation to all of them for this gratuitous insult to the commanding officer? Not that I took it personally, it was the principle, the principle of respect for command. That principle was dead when I came aboard that ship but I brought it to life and I nagged and I crabbed and I bitched and I hollered but by God I made it stick while I was the captain. And as I say—like the Silexes. It wasn't only the Silexes, it was a matter of respect, when I ask a sailor a question I want a straight answer and nobody's going to get away with shifty evasions if I have to hold a court of inquiry for a week. What do I care for strawberries? It was a question of principle, pilfering is pilfering, and on my ship—not that we had so many treats, either. With those slow-motion mess treasurers of ours—not like when I was an ensign, believe me, they made me jump sure enough—when we did get something pleasant like strawberries once in a blue moon it was an outrage not to have another helping if I felt like it, and I wasn't going to let them get away with that, and I didn't, by God, there was no more of that again on that ship. And so, as I say— Kay, how many of these things have I covered? I can only do this roughly from memory, but you ask me specific questions and I'll tackle them one by one.

(*During this speech* GREENWALD *strolls to his desk and leans against it, listening respectfully. The* COURT MEMBERS *stare at* QUEEG *and at each other and at their wrist watches after a while.* CHALLEE *slouches, biting his nails.*)

GREENWALD. It was a very thorough and complete answer, Commander, thank you. (*Goes to* STENOGRAPHER.) May I have exhibit twelve?

(STENOGRAPHER *hands him a glossy black photostat.*) Commander, I show you an authenticated copy of a fitness report you wrote on Lieutenant Maryk, dated 1 July 1944. Do you recognize it as such?

QUEEG. (*Takes paper, glances at it. Grumpily*) Yes.

GREENWALD. By that date, had the following incidents already occurred: the water shortage, the Silex investigation, the suspension of movies—among others?

QUEEG. (*Hesitates.*) Well, by then, yes, I think.

GREENWALD. Please read to the court your comment of 1 July on Lieutenant Maryk.

QUEEG. (*Stares at the paper. In a choked voice*) Naturally, not being vindictive, I don't write down every single thing—a fitness report goes into a man's record, and I—I try to go easy, I always have, I always will—

GREENWALD. I appreciate that, sir. Please read your comment.

QUEEG. (*Mumbling, hunched over, after a long pause.*) "This officer has if anything improved in his performance of duty since the last fitness report. He is consistently loyal, unflagging, thorough, courageous, and efficient. He is considered at present fully qualified for command of a twelve-hundred-ton DMS. His professional zeal and integrity set him apart as an outstanding example for other officers, reserve and regular alike. He cannot be too highly commended. He is recommended for transfer to the regular Navy."

GREENWALD. Thank you, Commander. No further questions.

(GREENWALD *walks to his desk and sits.* CHALLEE *stands slowly, like an old man with rheumatism. He approaches*

the witness stand, seems about to speak, then turns to
BLAKELY.)

CHALLEE. No cross-examination.

BLAKELY. You are excused, Commander.

(*Exit* QUEEG *slowly.*)

GREENWALD. Defense rests. (*Sits.*)

BLAKELY. Is the judge advocate ready to present his argument?

CHALLEE. Sir, I believe I'll waive the argument.

BLAKELY. No argument at all?

CHALLEE. If it please the court, I'm at a loss to discuss the case the defense has presented. I have nothing to refute. It's no case at all. It has nothing to do with the charge or the specification. The defense counsel's very first question in this trial was, "Commander, have you ever heard the expression, Old Yellowstain?" That was the key to his entire strategy—which was simply to twist the proceedings around so that the accused would become not Maryk but Commander Queeg. He's dragged out every possible vicious and malicious criticism of the commander from the other witnesses, and forced Queeg to defend himself against them in open court, on the spur of the moment, without advice of counsel, without any of the normal privileges and safeguards of an accused man under naval law. Can this court possibly endorse the precedent that a captain who doesn't please his underlings can be deposed by them? And that the captain's only recourse afterward is to be placed on the witness stand at a general court-martial to answer every petty gripe and justify all his command decisions to a hostile lawyer taking the part of his insubordinate inferiors? Such a precedent is nothing but a blank check for mutiny. It is the absolute destruction of the chain of command. However all this doesn't worry me sir. I'm confident that this court hasn't been impressed by such shyster tactics, I know the court is going to reject this cynical play on its emotions, this insult to its intelligence, and find the specification proven by the facts. I've only this to say, sir. Whatever the verdict on the accused, I formally recommend that defense counsel Greenwald be reprimanded by this court for conduct unbecoming an officer of the Navy—and that this reprimand be made part of his record. (*Sits.*)

BLAKELY. Defense counsel—closing argument?

GREENWALD. (*Rises, stands by his desk.*) Please the court, I undertook the defense of the accused very reluctantly, and only at the urging of the judge advocate that no other defense counsel was available. I was reluctant because I knew that the only possible defense was to show in court the mental incompetence of an officer of the Navy. It has been the most unpleasant duty I've ever had to perform. Once having undertaken it, I did what I could to win an acquittal. I thought this was my duty, both as defense counsel appointed by the Navy, and as a member of the bar. (*Comes forward slowly.*) Let me make only one thing clear. It is not, and never has been, the contention of the defense that Commander Queeg is a coward. The entire case of the defense rests on the assumption that no man who rises to command of a United States naval ship can possibly be a coward. And that therefore, if he commits questionable acts under fire the explanation must lie elsewhere. The court saw the bearing of Captain Queeg on the stand. The court can picture what his bearing must have been at the height of a typhoon. On that basis the court will decide the fate of the accused. (*Sits.*)

BLAKELY. Before recessing, the court will rule on the recommendation to reprimand.
    (COURT MEMBERS *write their votes and pass papers to him. He glances through papers and tears them up.*)
    Lieutenant Greenwald.

GREENWALD. (*Rises, comes to Center stage at attention.*) Yes, sir.

BLAKELY. Lieutenant, this has been a strange and tragic trial. You have conducted your case with striking ingenuity. The judge advocate's remark about "shyster tactics" was an unfortunate personal slur. But your conduct has been puzzling, and it does raise questions. With talent goes responsibility. Has your conduct here been responsible, Lieutenant Greenwald? The reprimand, if there's to be one, must come from your own conscience. Counsel's words and acts are privileged within the broad limits of contempt of court. Court finds defense counsel has not been in contempt. Recommendation to reprimand denied. (*Rings bell.*) Recess.

(*Exit* ALL *but* MARYK *and* GREENWALD.)

MARYK. What happens now?

GREENWALD. That's the ball game.

MARYK. When do we find out?

GREENWALD. If it's an acquittal, you'll find out in an hour or so. If it isn't they may not publish the findings for weeks.

MARYK. Meantime would I be confined?

GREENWALD. No, hardly.

MARYK. What do you think?

GREENWALD. I'd stick around for an hour or so.

MARYK. You were terrific.

GREENWALD. Thanks.

MARYK. You murdered Queeg.

GREENWALD. Yes, I murdered him.

MARYK. I'm grateful to you. Win or lose.

GREENWALD. Okay.

MARYK. What's the matter?

GREENWALD. Not a thing.

MARYK. You bothered by what Challee said? Or Blakely?

GREENWALD. Why should I be? I had a job to do. I did it. That's all.

MARYK. That's the spirit. Look. I want to ask your advice.

GREENWALD. What now?

MARYK. Tom Keefer's throwing a party tonight at the Fairmont Hotel. This morning he got a thousand-buck check —advance on his novel.

GREENWALD. Bully for him. I hope he sells a million copies, and wins the Pulitzer Prize, the Nobel Prize, and the Congressional Medal of Honor, and gets his bust in the Hall of Fame. That'll wrap this thing up in a pink ribbon.

MARYK. We're both invited to the party.

GREENWALD. What!

MARYK. Well, I know what you probably think. But hell, one way or another it's all over. I don't know what I'd have done in Tom's place.

GREENWALD. You'd go to Keefer's party?

MARYK. Tom's always called me a good-natured slob. I'll go if you will. If you think we should.

GREENWALD. (*Staring at him*) All right, maybe we'll both go and help Mr. Keefer celebrate.

BLACKOUT

(*Drunken singing of many male voices in the darkness, "I've Got Sixpence."*)

ACT TWO

Scene II

THE SCENE: *The scene is the private dining room in the Fairmont Hotel. A long table has been moved on. It is covered with a green cloth and a garland of flowers is stretched along the front. A green traveler has been pulled across the stage about half way into the courtroom. The table is stacked with bottles of champagne, glasses, and a huge cake baked in the form of a book.*

Seven officers in blues are grouped around the table, including MARYK, KEITH, *and* KEEFER. *They are* ALL *pretty drunk. They are sitting at various angles, waving glasses and bottles, and trying to drown each other out in the singing of "I've Got Sixpence."* KEITH *is trying desperately to sing, all alone, "Bell Bottom Trousers."* KEEFER *and* MARYK *tell him he is singing the wrong song and finally get him to join in their singing of "Sixpence."* GREENWALD *enters stage Left, unnoticed by the group, and stands silently watching their party.* KEEFER *glances off and sees* GREENWALD *standing there.*

KEEFER. Quiet! Quiet! All right, *QUIET*, you drunken bums of the *Caine!* Here he is! The guest of honor! Fill glasses! A toast to the conquering hero! Greenwald the Magnificent! The man who won the acquittal!

(*One of the members of the party walks over to* GREEN-
WALD *and takes him by the arm and moves* GREENWALD
closer to the table.)

GREENWALD. Party's pretty far along, hey?

KEEFER. A toast I say! To Lieutenant—

KEITH. Make it rhyme, Tom! Like you did at the ship's
party!

ALL. Yes, yes. That's right. Rhymes! Rhymes! A toast in
rhyme.

MARYK. (*To* GREENWALD.) He makes 'em up as he goes
along.

KEITH. You've never heard anything like it.

MARYK. Come on, Tom.

KEITH. Rhymes!

KEEFER. Well. I'm a bit drunk to be doing Thomas the
Rhymer tonight— But, to honor this great man, I'll try my
best. Fill your glasses, I say!
> To Lieutenant Barney Greenwald,
> Who fought with might and main.
> The terror of judge advocates,
> The massive legal brain.
> > (*They* ALL *cheer.*)
> Who hit the Navy where it lived
> And made it writhe with pain.
> Who sees through brass and gold stripes
> Like so much cellophane.
> > (*They* ALL *cheer.*)
> The man who licked the regulars
> Right on their own terrain,
> Who wrought the great deliverance
> For the galley-slaves of the *Caine*.
> > (*They* ALL *cheer.*)
> And gave us all the Fifth Freedom—
> Freedom from Old Yellowstain!

(*They* ALL *cheer. Then "Speech, Barney, speech, etc."*)

GREENWALD. No, no, no. I'm drunker'n any of you. I've been out drinking with the judge advocate—trying to get him to take back some of the dirty names he called me—finally got him to shake hands on the ninth whiskey sour—maybe the tenth—

MARYK. That's good.

GREENWALD. Had to talk loud 'n' fast, Steve— I played pretty dirty pool, you know, in court—poor Jack Challee— (*Peers blearily at cake.*) What's this?

KEEFER. It's a double celebration.

GREENWALD. Cake baked like a book—

KEEFER. A thousand bucks came in the mail today. Advance on my novel.

GREENWALD. Very nice. (*Reads icing.*) *Multitudes, Multitudes,* by Thomas Keefer— I got something in the mail, too.

MARYK. What, Barney?

GREENWALD. Medical okay. Orders back to my squadron. Sailing tomorrow.

(*They* ALL *cheer.*)

MARYK. That's great.

GREENWALD. A thousand bucks. Guess I ought to return the celebrated author's toast, at that— Li'l speech. —Thanks for that elegant poem, Mr. Keefer. War novel, isn't it?

KEEFER. What else?

GREENWALD. I assume you give the Navy a good pasting?

KEEFER. I don't think Public Relations would clear it, at any rate.

GREENWALD. Someone should show up these stodgy, stupid Prussians. Who's the hero, you?

KEEFER. Well, any resemblance, you know, is purely accidental—

(*A few laughs.*)

GREENWALD. 'Course I'm warped, and I'm drunk, but it suddenly seems to me that if I wrote a war novel I'd try to make a hero out of Old Yellowstain.

(ALL *whoop loudly.*)

No, I'm serious, I would. Tell you why. Tell you how I'm warped. I'm a Jew, guess most of you know that. Jack Challee said I used smart Jew-lawyer tactics—course he took it back, apologized, after I told him a few things about the case he never knew. Well, anyway—the reason I'd make Old Yellowstain a hero is on account of my mother, little gray-headed Jewish lady, fat. Well, sure you guys all have mothers, but they wouldn't be in the same bad shape mine would if we'd of lost this war. See, the Germans aren't kidding about the Jews. They're cooking us down to soap over there. They think we're vermin and should be 'sterminated and our corpses turned into something useful. Granting the premise—being warped, I don't, but granting the premise—soap is as good an idea as any. But I just can't cotton to the idea of my mom melted down to a bar of soap.

(*One of the* OFFICERS, *drunker than the rest, mutters maudlinly something ad lib:* "What's all this got to do with Old Yellowstain?" *or words to that effect. The* OTHERS *swiftly quiet him.* GREENWALD *rides over the interruption.*)

Now I'm coming to Old Yellowstain. Coming to him. See, Mr. Keefer, while I was studying law, and you were writing your short stories for national magazines, and little Willie here was on the playing fields of Princeton, why, all that time these birds we call regulars, these stuffy stupid Prussians, they were standing guard on this fat, dumb, and happy country of ours. 'Course they were doing it for dough, same as everybody does what they do. Question is in the last anal—last analysis, what do you do for dough? You and me, for dough, were advancing our free little non-Prussian careers. So, when all hell broke loose and the Germans started running out of soap and figured, well, time to come over and melt down old Mrs. Greenwald, who's gonna stop 'em? Not her boy Barney. Can't stop a Nazi with a lawbook. So, I dropped the law-books, and ran to learn how to fly. Stout fellow. Mean-time, and it took a year and a half before I was any good, who was keeping Mama out of the soap dish? Tom Keefer? Communication school. Willie Keith? Midship-man school. Old Yellowstain, maybe? Why yes, even poor sad Queeg. And most of them not sad at all, fellows, a lot of them sharper boys than any of us, don't kid yourself, you can't be good in the Army or Navy unless you're god-damn good. Though maybe not up on Proust, 'n' *Finnegan's Wake,* 'n' all.

MARYK. Barney, forget it, it's all over, let's enjoy the din-ner—

GREENWALD. Steve, this dinner's a phony. You're guilty. Course you're only half guilty. There's another guy who's stayed very neatly out of the picture. The guy who started the whole idea that Queeg was a dangerous para-noiac—who argued you into it for half a year—who invented the nickname "Old Yellowstain"—who kept feed-ing you those psychiatry books—who pointed out Article 184 and kept hammering it at you—

KEEFER. Now wait a minute—

GREENWALD. Oh, had to drag it out of Steve, Mister Keefer. Big dumb fisherman, tried to tell me it was all his own idea. Doesn't know the difference between a para-noid and an anthropoid. But you knew. Told him his medical log was a clinical picture of a paranoid. Advised him to go to Halsey. Offered to go with him. Didn't get cold feet till you stood outside Halsey's cabin on the *New Jersey*. Then ducked, and been ducking ever since.

KEEFER. I don't know where you got all this, but—

GREENWALD. Biggest favor you could have done Steve, so far as winning an acquittal went, though I doubt you realized it. But if there's a guilty party at this table, it's you. If you hadn't filled Steve Maryk's thick head full of paranoia and Article 184, why he'd have got Queeg to come north, or he'd have helped the poor bastard pull through to the south, and the *Caine* wouldn't have been yanked out of action in the hottest part of the war. That's your contribution to the good old U.S.A., my friend. Pulling a minesweeper out of the South Pacific when it was most needed. That, and *Multitudes, Multitudes.*

KEEFER. Just a minute—you're really drunk—

GREENWALD. 'Scuse me, I'm all finished, Mister Keefer. I'm up to the toast. Here's to you. You bowled a perfect score. You went after Queeg and got him. You kept your own skirts all white and starchy. You'll publish your novel proving that the Navy stinks, and you'll make a million dollars and marry Hedy Lamarr. So you won't mind a li'l verbal reprimand from me, what does it mean? I defended Steve because I found out the wrong guy was on trial. Only way I could defend him was to murder Queeg for you. I'm sore that I was pushed into that spot, and ashamed of what I did, and thass why I'm drunk. Queeg deserved better at my hands. I owed him a favor, don't you see? He stopped Hermann Goering from washing his fat behind with my mother. So I'm not going to eat your dinner, Mister Keefer, or drink your wine, but simply make my toast and go. Here's to you, Mister *Caine's* favorite author, and here's to your book.

(GREENWALD *throws the wine in* KEEFER'S *face. Shocked murmurs.*)

You can wipe for the rest of your life, mister. You'll never wipe off that yellow stain.

MARYK. Barney—

GREENWALD. See you in Tokyo, you mutineer. (*He staggers out.*)

END OF PLAY

1